Prentice Hall

MATHEMATICS
Course 2

Progress Monitoring
Assessments

Boston, Massachusetts • Chandler, Arizona • Glenview, Illinois • Upper Saddle River, New Jersey

ISBN-13: 978-0-13-372196-6
ISBN-10: 0-13-372196-5

3 4 5 6 7 8 9 10   V012   13 12 11 10

Table of Contents

To the Teacher:

During the school year, you assess how students are learning in your classroom using various types of assessments. Prentice Hall's *Progress Monitoring Assessments* provides a clear path to adequate yearly progress through systematic testing and recommendations for remediation.

Formative Assessments

When you give tests that help you identify students' strengths and weaknesses, your assessments are considered formative assessments. The results of these tests serve as a guide in planning and adjusting curriculum to assist struggling students and enhance all students' learning. There are several assessments and related activities in this book to assist you.

Screening Test

Before launching into the curriculum, you need to know how well your students read and how proficient they are in basic computation and problem-solving skills. Use the Screening Test to measure student readiness for your course.

Benchmark Tests

Proficiency testing is at the heart of progress monitoring and student achievement. At specified intervals throughout the year, give Benchmark Tests to evaluate student progress toward mastery of essential content.

Test-Taking Strategies Practice

Since a critical factor of assessment is to provide opportunities for students to learn better, use the Test-Taking Strategies Practice pages to investigate problem-solving strategies and strengthen students' application of these strategies with problems of varying complexity.

Standardized Test Practice

Since the NAEP, SAT 10, ITBS, and TerraNova tests are common assessments at high school, use these pages to acquaint students with topics, question formats, and practice. The activities and practice provided on these pages will allow students to be less anxious when they take these high stakes assessments for evaluation purposes.

Summative Assessments

When you give tests, usually at the end of a quarter or year, and the goal of the assessment is to evaluate mastery, your assessments are considered summative assessments. There are several assessments and related activities in this book to assist you. Quarter Tests, Mid-Course Tests, and Final Tests are available at two levels. The regular levels are designed to measure mastery of content over a span of chapters with the rigor presented in the lessons and exercises of the Student Edition. The below level forms are provided to support less-proficient readers, beginning English-language learners, and other struggling students. The problems meet the same mastery of content, but contain more visual support and fewer problems.

Assessment Support

Providing clear and supportive feedback to students is critical to progress monitoring, so use the comprehensive reports and answer keys provided in this book to map student results and follow-up with relevant remediation assignments.

Screening Test

1. What is the place value of the underlined digit in the following number?

    40,<u>3</u>21

    A ones

    B tens

    C hundreds

    D thousands

2. Which number can be written as *six and four fifths*?

    A 6.45

    B $6\frac{4}{5}$

    C $\frac{64}{5}$

    D $60 + 4 + 5$

3. Which fraction is less than $\frac{7}{10}$?

    A $\frac{1}{2}$

    B $\frac{3}{4}$

    C $\frac{4}{5}$

    D $\frac{9}{12}$

4. Which benchmarks can be used to estimate the following sum?

    $\frac{4}{7} + \frac{19}{20}$

    A $\frac{1}{3} + \frac{1}{2}$

    B $\frac{1}{4} + \frac{3}{4}$

    C $1 + 1$

    D $\frac{1}{2} + 1$

5. Add.

    $3,567 + 10,298$

    A 13,775

    B 13,855

    C 13,865

    D 14,855

6. Subtract.

    $41,304 - 25,877$

    A 14,427

    B 15,427

    C 16,503

    D 24,533

7. Add.

$$34\frac{4}{5} + 15\frac{3}{5}$$

A $49\frac{7}{5}$

B $49\frac{7}{10}$

C $50\frac{2}{5}$

D $50\frac{7}{10}$

8. Subtract. Express your answer in simplest form.

$$17\frac{5}{8} - 12\frac{3}{8}$$

A $5\frac{1}{4}$

B $5\frac{1}{8}$

C $5\frac{2}{8}$

D $5\frac{2}{16}$

9. Add.

$$71.7 + 1.34$$

A 73.04

B 85.1

C 205.7

D 851

10. Subtract.

$$42.3 - 24.67$$

A 16.67

B 17.36

C 17.63

D 18.67

11. Multiply.

$$27 \cdot 45$$

A 1,125

B 1,215

C 1,225

D 1,315

12. Divide.

$$688 \div 4$$

A 157

B 162

C 172

D 197

13. There are 354 students coming to the spring dinner dance. If each dinner table can seat 8 students, how many tables will be needed for the dinner dance?

A 42 tables

B 43 tables

C 44 tables

D 45 tables

14. A recipe calls for 2 cups of sugar, 2 eggs, 3 cups of flour, and 5 cups of milk. What is the ratio of sugar to flour?

  A 2 to 5

  B 3 to 2

  C 2 to 2

  D 2 to 3

15. Which value is an odd number?

  A 3,350

  B 5,114

  C 8,461

  D 213,110

16. Which is *not* a factor of 36?

  A 3

  B 9

  C 12

  D 16

17. Which of the following number sentences demonstrates the Commutative Property?

  A $4 + (5 + 6) = (4 + 5) + 6$

  B $7 + 0 = 7$

  C $7 + 3 = 3 + 7$

  D $6(4 + 3) = 24 + 18$

18. If an airline flight attendant wants to know if a suitcase is too heavy to carry on board the plane, which of the following will she need to measure?

  A the height of the suitcase

  B the weight of the suitcase

  C the capacity of the suitcase

  D the length of the suitcase

19. Which measuring tool would make the most sense to use when determining the length of a classroom?

  A a meter stick

  B a compass

  C a balance scale

  D a measuring cup

20. The perimeter of a rectangle, P, may be found using the formula $2l + 2w = P$, where $l =$ length and $w =$ width. What is the perimeter of the rectangle shown below?

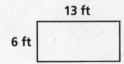

  A 19 ft

  B 38 ft

  C 57 ft

  D 78 ft

21. What is the area of a square with a side length of 15 inches? Use the formula $A = lw$.

  A 30 in.^{2}

  B 60 in.^{2}

  C 225 in.^{2}

  D 360 in.^{2}

22. Tim lives 6 blocks from his school. He measured the time it takes him to walk to school. Which would be the *best* unit for Tim to use to express his time?

  A seconds

  B minutes

  C feet

  D hours

23. A bicycle tire has what shape?

  A sphere

  B circle

  C oval

  D square

24. Which angle appears to be an acute angle?

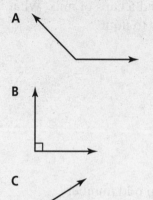

25. Which statement is *not* true?

  A All squares are rectangles.

  B All parallelograms are rectangles.

  C All squares are rhombuses.

  D All squares have 4 congruent sides.

26. Which solid shape can be formed by the following plane shapes?

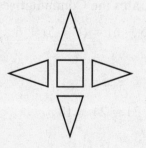

  A triangular prism

  B cube

  C square pyramid

  D cone

27. Which shape is used to make the *bases* of the following solid figure?

A squares

B triangles

C rectangles

D rhombus

28. What type of data display is shown below?

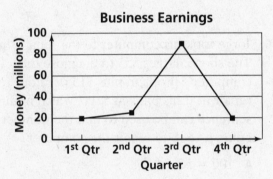

A bar graph

B table

C line graph

D histogram

29. How many students play soccer?

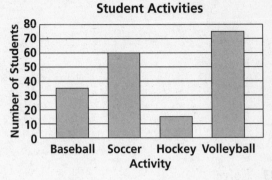

A 15 students

B 35 students

C 60 students

D 75 students

30. A delivery person receives several uniform items when he is hired. If he has 3 shirts and 2 pairs of shorts to choose from, how many different combinations of uniforms can he make?

A 3

B 5

C 6

D 9

31. The letters of the word GEORGIA are placed in a box. What is the probability that a vowel will be picked from the box?

A $\frac{3}{4}$

B $\frac{3}{7}$

C $\frac{4}{7}$

D $\frac{5}{7}$

32. What is the next number in the pattern?

2, 5, 9, 14, 20, ...

A 25

B 27

C 28

D 30

33. Solve.

$2x - 5 = 19$

A $x = 7$

B $x = 10$

C $x = 12$

D $x = 15$

34. Annie has worked 3 more than 5 times the number of hours that Sam has worked. Which algebraic expression represents this statement, where x is the number of hours Sam worked?

A $3x + 5$

B $3 + 5x$

C $8x$

D $5x - 3x$

35. Which point is represented by the ordered pair $(4, 2)$?

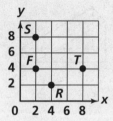

A F

B R

C S

D T

36. Jorge took his computer to the repair shop. The shop charges $55 to diagnose the computer's problem plus $15 per hour to repair it. If his bill was $100, which number sentence can be used to find the number of hours it took to repair the computer?

A $100 = 55x + 15$

B $100 = 55 - 15x$

C $100 = 55 + 15x$

D $100 = 55x - 15$

STOP

Benchmark Test 1

1. In which of the following situations would it be most useful to use an estimate instead of an exact number?

   A specifying the number of people allowed in an elevator

   B specifying the number of cars it takes to fill a parking lot

   C specifying the number of hours worked in a week

   D specifying the number of people attending a World Series baseball game

2. Which is a reasonable estimate for the mass of your math textbook?

   F 2 mg

   G 20 g

   H 2 kg

   J 20 kg

3. Which is the closest estimate of the product of 3.85 and 7.14?

   A 21

   B 24

   C 25

   D 27

4. Which measurement would *best* be described using meters?

   F the distance from Honolulu, Hawaii, to Boston, Massachusetts

   G the height of a roller coaster

   H the length of a parrot's tail feather

   J the thickness of a hair on your head

5. Kim's dog Ladyhawk had four puppies. Kim named each puppy and determined its mass. She recorded the information on a chart.

   Ladyhawk's Puppies

Puppy	Mass
Kip	398 g
Red	0.38 kg
Sparky	0.42 kg
Sleepy	419 g

   Which puppy has the greatest mass?

   A Kip   **C** Sleepy

   B Red   **D** Sparky

6. Jason has a 2-liter pitcher of lemonade and some 250-milliliter glasses. How many servings of lemonade can he serve using these glasses?

   F 6

   G 8

   H 10

   J 12

7. The list below shows the low temperatures for Detroit, Michigan, for the months of October through February.

   10°F, −5°F, −8°F, −22°F, and −14°F

   Which lists shows the temperatures ordered from least to greatest?

   A 10°F, −5°F, −8°F, −22°F, −14°F

   B −5°F, −8°F, −22°F, −14°F, 10°F

   C −5°F, −8°F, 10°F, −14°F, −22°F

   D −22°F, −14°F, −8°F, −5°F, 10°F

8. Which of the letters on the number line below represents an integer that is greater than −3 but less than 2?

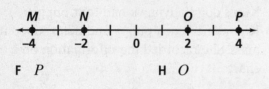

F *P*   H *O*

G *N*   J *M*

9. A coach listed the rushing yards per quarter for each of his running backs. Which two players led the team in rushing yards during the 4th quarter?

Rushing Yards per Quarter

Player	1st Quarter	2nd Quarter	3rd Quarter	4th Quarter
Thomas	18	−34	22	−12
Ji	10	3	0	6
Jamison	−16	22	8	−9
Griffin	19	12	6	−8
Lopez	15	16	−20	9
Grant	5	6	3	7
Moseley	6	12	−19	36

A Griffin and Ji

B Moseley and Thomas

C Grant and Lopez

D Lopez and Moseley

10. What is the mean of the following set of data?

15, 15, 22, 10, 18, 22

F 13

G 15

H 17

J 22

11. While on a one-week vacation at the beach, Margot recorded these daily noon temperatures.

85°, 75°, 98°, 102°, 80°, 95°, and 98°

For how many days was the daily noon temperature greater than the average weekly noon temperature?

A 2 days

B 3 days

C 4 days

D 5 days

12. Listed below are the salaries for the employees in one department of a company.

Salaries

$34,000	$21,500	$89,000
$36,400	$24,000	$24,000
$48,300	$28,000	$39,000
$29,500	$33,500	$32,600
$18,250	$42,700	$49,600

Which salary is *most* likely to be considered an outlier?

F $18,250

G $32,600

H $49,600

J $89,000

13. An art museum offers seven tours during the day. The list below shows the number of people on each tour during one day. What is the mean number of people per tour?

45, 32, 65, 43, 32, 62, 64

A 32

B 43

C 45

D 49

14. The number of snowy January days for a certain city was recorded over a 10-year period.

$$11, 3, 5, 9, 5, 10, 9, 7, 9, 2$$

What is the mode of this snow data?

F 5

G 7

H 8

J 9

15. The table below shows the average monthly precipitation in Seattle, Washington, for the months of September through March. Find the median of the precipitation data.

Seattle Precipitation

Month	Precipitation (in.)
September	1.9
October	3.3
November	5.7
December	6.0
January	5.4
February	4.0
March	3.7

A 3.0 inches

B 4.0 inches

C 5.0 inches

D 6.0 inches

16. Which of the following is *not* a way of expressing 4^3?

F four raised to the third power

G $4 \times 4 \times 4$

H the product of four and three

J 64

17. Simplify.

$$2^3 \cdot (9 - 6)^4$$

A 216

B 324

C 648

D 864

18. There are 2 rabbits in a field. The rabbit population doubles every 3 months. Which expression represents the number of rabbits in the field after 12 months?

F $2 \times 3 \times 12$

G 2^5

H 3^4

J $\left(\dfrac{12}{3}\right)^2$

19. Which of the following represents 2.83×10^6 written in standard notation?

A 283,000

B 2,830,000

C 28,300,000

D 283,000,000

20. Which of the following represents the scale factor of 20,000 to 40,000 in scientific notation?

F 2×10^3 to 4×10^3

G 2×10^4 to 4×10^4

H 20×10^3 to 40×10^3

J 200×10^2 to 400×10^2

21. The collection of the Smithsonian's National Portrait Gallery in Washington, D.C., includes 18,600 works. In 1999, 432,000 people visited the gallery. Express in scientific notation the number of works and the number of visitors.

A 1.86×10^2; 4.32×10^3

B 1.86×10^3; 4.32×10^4

C 1.86×10^4; 4.32×10^5

D 1.86×10^5; 4.32×10^6

22. The members of a marching band line up into rows with an equal number of band members in each row. If there are 8 rows, which number listed below could be the number of members in the band?

F 100

G 120

H 165

J 194

23. Which is the missing digit that will make this number divisible by 9?

3,4■5

A 1   **C** 6

B 3   **D** 9

24. Which of the following is *not* an accurate divisibility test?

F If a number is divisible by 9 then it is also divisible by 3.

G If a number is divisible by 10 then it is also divisible by 2 and 5.

H If a number is divisible by 6 then it is also divisible by 2 and 3.

J If a number is divisible by 2 and 4 then it is also divisible by 8.

25. John would prefer to have a prime number greater than 25 on the back of his football jersey. Which number listed below could John choose?

A 23

B 27

C 33

D 37

26. What is the prime factorization of 108?

F 2×54

G $2^2 \times 27$

H $2^2 \times 3^3$

J $2^3 \times 3^2$

27. There are 1,764 computers loaded onto n trucks. If each truck contains the same number of computers, which could *not* be the number of trucks used?

A 4 trucks

B 6 trucks

C 8 trucks

D 9 trucks

28. Which of the following fractions is *not* equivalent to $\frac{2}{3}$?

F $\frac{4}{9}$

G $\frac{8}{12}$

H $\frac{10}{15}$

J $\frac{4}{6}$

Name _____ Class _____ Date _____

29. Roberto rode his bike for 36 minutes before getting a flat tire. He then walked 24 minutes. What fraction of his time was spent walking?

A $\frac{1}{5}$

B $\frac{2}{5}$

C $\frac{3}{5}$

D $\frac{2}{3}$

30. A poll found that 63 percent of Americans get less than eight hours of sleep a night. What fraction of a day does this number of hours represent?

F $\frac{1}{8}$

G $\frac{1}{4}$

H $\frac{1}{3}$

J $\frac{2}{3}$

31. Which of the following number sentences is true?

A $\frac{5}{8} > \frac{3}{4}$

B $\frac{3}{9} > \frac{1}{3}$

C $\frac{5}{6} > \frac{2}{3}$

D $\frac{3}{5} < \frac{4}{10}$

32. Four students painted a mural on a concrete wall in the schoolyard. Maggie painted $\frac{3}{8}$ of the mural; Pedro painted $\frac{5}{16}$ of the mural, Laurel painted $\frac{1}{4}$ of the mural, and Zach painted $\frac{1}{16}$ of the mural. Which student did the most painting?

F Maggie

G Pedro

H Laurel

J Zach

33. Which fraction is equal to $0.\overline{4}$?

A $\frac{2}{5}$

B $\frac{4}{10}$

C $\frac{2}{3}$

D $\frac{4}{9}$

34. Which of the following lists of numbers is in order from least to greatest?

F $\frac{4}{5}, -2, 0, -\frac{1}{3}, 0.75$

G $-\frac{1}{3}, \frac{4}{5}, 0.75, 0, -2$

H $-2, 0, -\frac{1}{3}, 0.75, \frac{4}{5}$

J $-2, -\frac{1}{3}, 0, 0.75, \frac{4}{5}$

35. The sum of two fractions is $4\frac{5}{8}$. Which of the following also describes this sum?

    A 4.0625

    B $\frac{37}{8}$

    C 4.58

    D $\frac{45}{8}$

36. Brandy plays softball in a softball league. Last year she had 60 hits during 150 times at bat. What was Brandy's batting average last year?

    F 0.150

    G 0.375

    H 0.400

    J 0.425

STOP

Benchmark Test 2

1. Marco weighs $137\frac{1}{4}$ pounds. Carlos weighs $165\frac{2}{3}$ pounds. How much more does Carlos weigh than Marco?

   A $28\frac{1}{7}$ lb

   B $28\frac{5}{12}$ lb

   C $32\frac{1}{7}$ lb

   D $32\frac{1}{12}$ lb

2. Gina ran $5\frac{3}{4}$ km on Monday, $6\frac{1}{12}$ km on Tuesday, $5\frac{1}{3}$ km on Wednesday, and $6\frac{4}{5}$ km on Thursday. About how many kilometers did Gina run in all?

   F 22 km   H 26 km

   G 24 km   J 28 km

3. The table below shows the weight and length of three young manatees. About how much *total* weight did the manatees gain in the six-month period?

   Manatee Growth

Manatee	January 1 Weight (kg)	January 1 Length (m)	July 1 Weight (kg)	July 1 Length (m)
1	$35\frac{1}{2}$	$\frac{3}{4}$	$78\frac{1}{2}$	$1\frac{1}{2}$
2	$42\frac{3}{4}$	$\frac{7}{8}$	$85\frac{3}{4}$	$1\frac{3}{4}$
3	$41\frac{1}{3}$	$\frac{4}{5}$	$89\frac{1}{4}$	$1\frac{4}{5}$

   A 134 kg   C 186 kg

   B 139 kg   D 254 kg

4. The walking track at one fitness center is $\frac{2}{5}$ mile long. If Kara walks around the track 8 times, how many miles does Kara walk?

   F $1\frac{1}{5}$ mi

   G $3\frac{1}{5}$ mi

   H 8 mi

   J 20 mi

5. Jerry and his family drove from Somerville to Borne. Jerry's mother drove for $4\frac{4}{5}$ hours. Jerry slept for $\frac{1}{4}$ of that time. His sister slept for 2 hours. How much longer did Jerry's sister sleep than he did?

   A 48 minutes

   B 72 minutes

   C 122 minutes

   D 138 minutes

6. It takes Tom $2\frac{1}{4}$ hours to paint one classroom. Tom had $\frac{2}{3}$ of the job completed when he ran out of paint. Once he buys more paint, how much more time will it take Tom to finish painting the classroom?

   F $\frac{2}{3}$ hour

   G $\frac{3}{4}$ hour

   H $1\frac{1}{2}$ hours

   J $1\frac{7}{12}$ hours

7. Solve.

$$4\frac{1}{3} \div 3\frac{1}{4}$$

A $\frac{3}{4}$

B $1\frac{1}{3}$

C $\frac{1}{12}$

D 1

8. Water stations are evenly spaced throughout the course of a $26\frac{1}{5}$-mile marathon. If there are 15 water stations, how many miles apart are the water stations?

F $\frac{26}{75}$ miles

G $1\frac{11}{15}$ miles

H $1\frac{56}{75}$ miles

J $1\frac{31}{75}$ miles

9. In 1954, the runner Roger Bannister was the first to break the four-minute mile. He completed four $\frac{1}{4}$-mile laps in 3 minutes $59\frac{4}{10}$ seconds. What was his average time per lap?

A $39\frac{17}{20}$ seconds

B $49\frac{17}{20}$ seconds

C $59\frac{17}{20}$ seconds

D $69\frac{17}{20}$ seconds

10. How many $\frac{3}{4}$-in. pieces can be cut from a piece of wood that measures 8 ft 9 in.?

F 12 pieces

G 79 pieces

H 128 pieces

J 140 pieces

11. One of the heaviest cars on record is a limousine that weighs 3.3 tons. How many *pounds* does the limousine weigh?

A 3,000 pounds

B 3,300 pounds

C 6,000 pounds

D 6,600 pounds

12. When cycling, it is best to drink 20 ounces of water every fifteen minutes of cycling. How many *pints* of water should you drink every hour?
(Hint: 1 pint = 2 c and 1 c = 8 fl oz)

F $1\frac{1}{4}$ pints per hour

G 5 pints per hour

H $8\frac{3}{4}$ pints per hour

J 10 pints per hour

Name _____ Class _____ Date _____

13. Which word phrase can be modeled by the following algebraic expression?

$$4t - 9$$

A nine less than four times a number

B nine minus the product of four and a number

C the product of a number and four is less than nine

D four less nine times a number

14. During intermission at the ballet recital, Serena bought four glasses of lemonade. If c represents the amount Serena spent, which algebraic expression represents the cost of one glass of lemonade?

F $4c$

G $\dfrac{c}{4}$

H $c + 4$

J $c - 4$

15. Bill's job pays $12.75 per hour. Which algebraic expression represents Bill's pay, in dollars, for working h hours?

A $12.75 + h$

B $12.75 - h$

C $12.75h$

D $\dfrac{h}{12.75}$

16. A coach spent $975.84 on new uniforms for his team. If he bought uniforms for 16 players, how much did each uniform cost? Use x to represent the price of each uniform.

F $16x = 975.84$
   $x = \$53.75$

G $16x = 975.84$
   $x = \$60.99$

H $12x = 975.84$
   $x = \$81.32$

J $12x = 975.84$
   $x = \$72.98$

17. Solve the following equation for s.

$$\frac{s}{-36} = 8$$

A -288

B -144

C -4.5

D $-0.\overline{2}$

18. Twelve employees at a fruit company are packing mangos into boxes. Twenty-four mangos will fit in every box. If they have approximately 2,064 mangos to pack, how many boxes are needed?

F 86

G 122

H 288

J 172

19. Which sequence of steps should you perform on each side of the following equation to solve for x?

$$\frac{x}{8} + 4 = 13$$

A Multiply by 8 and then subtract 4.

B Subtract 13 and then multiply by 8.

C Subtract 4 and then divide by 8.

D Subtract 4 and then multiply by 8.

20. Which equation has a solution of 0.6?

F $3x - 0.5 = 2.0$

G $4x - 0.5 = 1.9$

H $1.3 + 2x = -1.1$

J $1.2 + 2x = 3.0$

21. If m is equal to 32.5, which expression will make the following equation true?

$$2.25 + \blacksquare = 8.75$$

A $\frac{5}{m}$

B $(m + 5)$

C $5(m)$

D $\frac{m}{5}$

22. Solve for p.

$$\frac{3}{5}p + 17 = 68$$

F 7

G 51

H 65

J 85

23. The student council is decorating the cafeteria for the homecoming dance. They have 120 carnations to use. They will use 15 carnations for the door decoration and the rest will go on the tables. If the students plan to use 5 carnations per table, how many tables are they decorating?

A 10

B 21

C 25

D 45

24. Dawit bought 5 packages of socks and one $18.00 T-shirt with his favorite soccer-team logo on it. His total bill was $73.00. How much did each package of socks cost?

F $11.00

G $12.25

H $15.00

J $18.20

25. Solve for x.

$$2x + 11 = 17$$

A 3

B $3\frac{1}{2}$

C $4\frac{1}{2}$

D 14

26. Jose wants to buy a pair of bowling shoes that are on sale for $37.50. He has a jar of nickels and a $20.00 bill. Which equation will help him figure out how many nickels he needs in order to have enough money to buy the bowling shoes?

F $0.05m + 20.00 = 37.50$

G $m + 20.00 = 37.50$

H $5m + 20 = 37.5$

J $5m + 2,000 = 375$

27. Tickets for a drama club performance cost $6.00 for adults and $2.00 for students. For one performance, club members sold 25 more adult tickets than student tickets. If the total amount of ticket sales for this performance was $1,198, how many of each type of ticket did they sell?

A 156 adult tickets, 131 student tickets

B 175 adult tickets, 150 student tickets

C 131 adult tickets, 106 student tickets

D 106 adult tickets, 131 student tickets

28. Which statement describes the inequality graphed below?

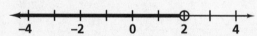

F $x > 2$

G $x \geq 2$

H $x \leq 2$

J $x < 2$

29. Which graph represents the solutions to the inequality $x \geq -3$?

30. To maintain his B average, Marc's score, s, on the next math quiz must be at least 88. Which inequality describes this situation?

F $s \leq 88$

G $s > 88$

H $s \geq 88$

J $s < 88$

31. Which graph represents the solutions to the inequality $-14t \leq 98$?

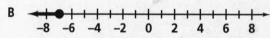

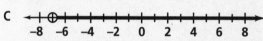

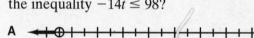

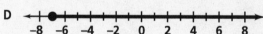

32. Solve the following inequality.

$$2x - 40 > 32$$

F $x \le -36$

G $x \le -8$

H $x > 36$

J $x > 72$

33. The costs for Ling's long-distance phone plan include a monthly connection fee of $15.00 plus a charge of $0.03 per minute for each call made. Ling does not want her monthly bill to exceed $30. Which inequality can she use to find the number of minutes of calls she can make each month?

A $15m + 3 < 30$

B $0.3m - 15 \le 30$

C $15 + 0.03(m) \le 30$

D $15m(0.03) \le 30$

Benchmark Test 3

1. Which ratio is in simplest form?

   A twenty-eight out of forty

   B 4 : 60

   C nine to fifty-three

   D $\frac{5}{30}$

2. There are 5 dogs, 8 cats, and 2 birds for sale at the pet store. What is the ratio in simplest form of birds to cats?

   F 8 to 5

   G 1 : 4

   H 4 : 1

   J 8 to 2

3. An adult blue whale may weigh 145 tons and grow to 100 feet long. Which of the following is the ratio of the weight to the length of a blue whale? Express the ratio in lowest terms.

   A $\frac{20}{29}$

   B $\frac{50}{72.5}$

   C 29 to 20

   D 145 : 100

4. Derek can type approximately 4,800 words in 2 hours 30 minutes. What is his average typing rate?

   F 32 words per minute

   G 48 words per minute

   H 32 words per hour

   J 48 words per hour

5. If a 21-ounce box of cereal costs $2.94, what is the unit price?

   A $0.11 per oz

   B $0.12 per oz

   C $0.13 per oz

   D $0.14 per oz

6. Sonja is shopping for apples. Which rate gives the lowest unit price for apples?

   F $\frac{\$0.89}{1 \text{ lb}}$

   G $\frac{\$1.55}{2 \text{ lb}}$

   H $\frac{\$3.15}{3 \text{ lb}}$

   J $\frac{\$3.89}{4 \text{ lb}}$

7. Which pair of ratios can form a proportion?

   A $\frac{1}{2}, \frac{7}{15}$

   B $\frac{2}{3}, \frac{9}{12}$

   C $\frac{3}{5}, \frac{7}{10}$

   D $\frac{7}{8}, \frac{21}{24}$

8. Solve the following proportion for x.

   $$\frac{4}{7} = \frac{16}{x}$$

   F 1.75

   G 9.2

   H 16

   J 28

9. Which ratio can form a proportion with the fraction $\frac{5}{8}$?

A $\frac{20}{36}$

B $\frac{15}{24}$

C $\frac{8}{5}$

D $\frac{16}{10}$

10. The two triangles shown below are similar. What is the measure of $\overline{FE}$?

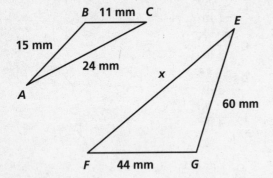

F 24 mm

G 96 mm

H 120 mm

J 216 mm

11. An office building casts a shadow that is 125 yards long. A 6-foot-tall man standing near the office building casts a shadow that is 15 feet long. How tall is the building?

A 50 ft

B 150 ft

C 250 ft

D 350 ft

12. Triangle ABC is similar to triangle XYZ. If the measure of angle B is 60°, what is the measure of angle Y?

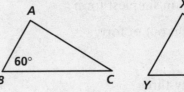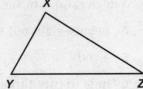

F 30°

G 60°

H 80°

J 100°

13. The scale on a map is $\frac{1}{4}$ inch : 50 miles. The distance between cities on the map is $6\frac{1}{2}$ inches. What is the actual distance between the two cities?

A 325 mi

B 650 mi

C 1,300 mi

D 1,500 mi

14. Clyde made a model of his favorite type of car. His model is 6 inches long, and the actual length of the car is 15 feet. What is the scale of Clyde's model?

F 1 in. : 15 in.

G 1 in. : 18 in.

H 1 in. : 24 in.

J 1 in. : 30 in.

15. Jose is remodeling his family's kitchen. He drew a blueprint of the kitchen with a scale of $\frac{1}{2}$ inch : 1 yard. What are the dimensions of his blueprint if the actual dimensions of the room are 15 feet × 21 feet?

A $\frac{1}{2}$ in. × 1 in.

B $2\frac{1}{2}$ in. × $3\frac{1}{2}$ in.

C 10 in. × 14 in.

D 15 in. × 21 in.

16. What is the value of the missing number?

$$\frac{6}{?} = \frac{30}{100}$$

F 20

G 30

H 40

J 60

17. You have twelve pairs of socks and nine pairs are white. What percent of your socks are white?

A 21%

B 54%

C 66%

D 75%

18. Which decimal is equivalent to 4.02%?

F 0.0402

G 0.402

H 4.02

J 402

19. Write $\frac{18}{25}$ as a percent.

A 36%

B 54%

C 72%

D 86%

20. Which of the following percents has the smallest value?

F $\frac{1}{4}$%

G $\frac{2}{5}$%

H 0.4%

J 2.5%

21. Which list is in order from least to greatest?

A 0.32, 7%, $\frac{4}{5}$, 10.2%

B 10.2%, 7%, 0.32, $\frac{4}{5}$

C 0.32, $\frac{4}{5}$, 7%, 10.2%

D 7%, 10.2%, 0.32, $\frac{4}{5}$

22. Oscar, Ian, Jesse, and Luis ordered three large pizzas. Each pizza had 8 slices. Of the pizza they ordered, Oscar ate 35%, Ian ate $\frac{1}{4}$, Jesse ate $\frac{3}{10}$, and Luis ate 10%. Who ate the *second most* pieces of pizza?

F Oscar

G Ian

H Jesse

J Luis

23. Which expression is equivalent to 0.52%?

A 0.0052

B 0.052

C $\frac{52}{1,000}$

D $\frac{5.2}{100}$

24. In one city the rainfall in July was 110% of the month's normal rainfall. If the normal rainfall is 3.2 inches, what was July's rainfall that year?

F 2.88 in.

G 3.52 in.

H 3.58 in.

J 4.32 in.

25. After Janet moved, her driving time to work became $1\frac{2}{5}$ times her previous driving time. What is this mixed number expressed as a percent?

A 104%

B 120%

C 140%

D 150%

26. 70% of what number is 42?

F 60

G 72

H 84

J 93

27. What percent of 35 is 21?

A 14%

B 21%

C 40%

D 60%

28. On Keith's most recent spelling test there were 55 questions. His grade was 80%. How many words did Keith spell correctly?

F 40 words

G 42 words

H 44 words

J 46 words

29. Fernando sells flowers at a flea market. One Saturday he sold a total of 740 flowers. The table below shows the percent of each type of flower that he sold.

Flower	Part of Whole
Roses	30%
Tulips	15%
Carnations	32%
Violets	5%
Daisies	18%

How many roses did Fernando sell?

A 222

B 247

C 300

D 405

30. Steve is painting a fence around his yard. He painted 60% of the fence yesterday. This morning he painted $\frac{2}{5}$ of the remaining fence. What percent of the fence is still unpainted?

F 16%

G 18%

H 24%

J 40%

31. Gina plans to buy a birdbath for her garden. The birdbath costs $79.95. The sales tax rate in her state is 8.25%. What will be the total cost of the birdbath?

A $73.35

B $86.55

C $88.20

D $91.55

32. Trey pays $34.25 for dinner. If he leaves a 15% tip, how much will he spend on dinner and the tip?

F $37.69

G $38.94

H $39.08

J $39.39

33. Amber bought a shirt on sale for $12. The original price was $15. Find the percent of discount.

A 20%

B 24%

C 27%

D 30%

34. A music store buys compact discs for $9.90 each. The store sells each disc for $14.65. What is the percent of markup?

F 34%

G 48%

H 52%

J 65%

35. Marco bags groceries. After six months on the job his pay increases from $5.25 per hour to $6.15 per hour. Find the percent increase in his hourly rate of pay.

A 9%

B 12%

C 15%

D 17%

36. Greg is paid a salary of $500.00 per month plus 15% commission on all the furniture sales in his department. How many dollars' worth of furniture does Greg's department need to sell this month for Greg to receive a $3,500.00 paycheck?

F $20,000

G $20,500

H $23,333

J $26,666

Benchmark Test 4

1. What is the measure of the supplement of an angle that measures 35°?

   A 55°

   B 65°

   C 145°

   D 155°

2. Which of the following angles measures 42°?

   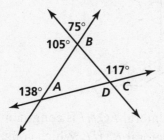

   F ∠A

   G ∠B

   H ∠C

   J ∠D

3. The complement of an unknown angle measures 57°. What is the supplement of the unknown angle?

   A 33°

   B 123°

   C 147°

   D 153°

4. The ramp shown below is installed by the front door of Lucy's school. What is the value of x?

   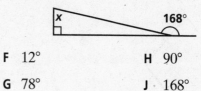

   F 12°   H 90°

   G 78°   J 168°

5. The smallest angle in a right triangle measures 36°. What is the measure of the second smallest angle in the triangle?

   A 46°

   B 48°

   C 52°

   D 54°

6. Which of the following triangles *cannot* have a 90° angle?

   F a scalene triangle

   G an equilateral triangle

   H an isosceles triangle

   J a right triangle

7. What type of quadrilateral is shown below?

   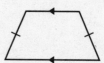

   A square

   B rhombus

   C trapezoid

   D parallelogram

8. Which of the following polygons is *not* a rhombus?

F

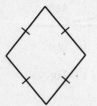

G

H

J

9. Which type of polygon does *not* include squares?

A parallelograms

B quadrilaterals

C rectangles

D trapezoids

10. Which of the following figures is *not* congruent to the figure below?

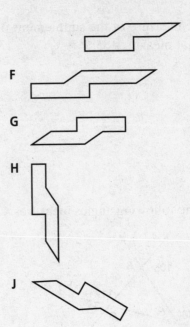

F

G

H

J

11. Quadrilateral *FGJH* is congruent to quadrilateral *RSUT*. Which congruence statement is true?

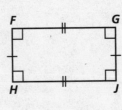

A $\overline{FG} \cong \overline{US}$

B $\overline{FH} \cong \overline{TU}$

C $\overline{GJ} \cong \overline{HJ}$

D $\overline{FG} \cong \overline{RS}$

12. If figure *ABCDE* is congruent to figure *LMNOP*, what is the length of $\overline{OP}$ and the measure of $\angle P$?

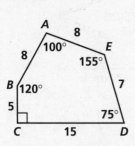 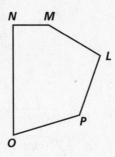

F   *OP* = 8; $m\angle P = 75°$

G   *OP* = 15; $m\angle P = 100°$

H   *OP* = 7; $m\angle P = 155°$

J   *OP* = 15; $m\angle P = 155°$

13. Karen surveyed 150 of her classmates to determine their favorite flavor of ice cream. How many students chose either chocolate or strawberry as their favorite flavor?

Favorite Ice Cream Flavors

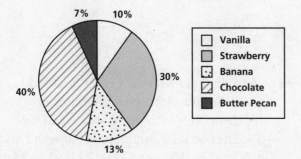

A   10 students

B   35 students

C   70 students

D   105 students

14. Which central angle measure represents 45% in a circle graph?

F   45°

G   153°

H   162°

J   400°

15. The results of a survey are displayed in a circle graph. One of the central angles measures 144°. If 500 people participated in the survey, how many people does this central angle represent?

A   144

B   200

C   244

D   300

16. A field is 100.2 meters long and 74.8 meters wide. Which of the following is the closest estimate of the area of the field?

F   350 m^2

G   5,625 m^2

H   7,500 m^2

J   10,000 m^2

17. A one-dollar bill has a length of 15.6 centimeters and a width of 6.6 centimeters. Which of the following is the closest estimate of the area of a one-dollar bill?

A   40 cm^2

B   80 cm^2

C   110 cm^2

D   140 cm^2

18. Each square in the diagram below represents 30 square miles. Which of the following is the closest estimate of the area of the shaded region?

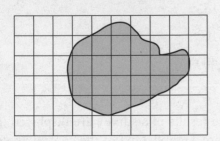

F 18 mi^2

G 21 mi^2

H 300 mi^2

J 540 mi^2

19. What is the area of the triangle shown below?

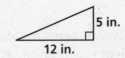

5 in.

12 in.

A 17 in.^{2}

B 30 in.^{2}

C 45 in.^{2}

D 60 in.^{2}

20. A diagonal parking space has the shape of a parallelogram. What is the area of the shaded parking space shown below?

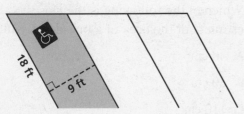

18 ft

9 ft

F 54 ft^2

G 81 ft^2

H 162 ft^2

J 180 ft^2

21. What is the approximate area of the sign shown below?

75 cm | NO PASSING ZONE

100 cm

A 2,500 cm^2

B 3,750 cm^2

C 5,750 cm^2

D 7,500 cm^2

22. In professional baseball, the circular pitcher's mound has a diameter of 18 feet. What is the circumference of the pitcher's mound? Use 3.14 as an approximation for π.

F 28.26 feet

G 32.78 feet

H 44.74 feet

J 56.52 feet

23. The Barringer Meteor Crater is located near Winslow, Arizona. This crater is approximately circular in shape and has a diameter of 1.2 kilometers. What is the area of Barringer Meteor Crater? Use 3.14 as an approximation for π.

A 1.13 km^2

B 2.36 km^2

C 3.24 km^2

D 4.52 km^2

24. Mr. Li placed a birdbath in the middle of his flower garden. The base of the birdbath is a circle. How much area is left in the garden for the flowers? Use 3.14 as an approximation for π.

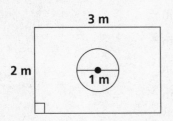

F 2.86 m^2 **H** 5.22 m^2

G 3.14 m^2 **J** 9.14 m^2

25. Which of the following is an irrational number?

A $\sqrt{4}$

B $\sqrt{6}$

C $0.44444444\ldots$

D $0.46464646\ldots$

26. Which of the following expressions has a value of 7?

F $\sqrt{7}$

G $\sqrt{14}$

H $\sqrt{49}$

J $\sqrt{81}$

27. A square tabletop has an area of 900 square inches. What is the length of the side of the tabletop?

A 30 in.

B 60 in.

C 150 in.

D 450 in.

28. What is the length of side k in the triangle below?

F 5 cm

G 5.5 cm

H 6 cm

J 6.5 cm

29. Ramon lives 12 miles due south of the swimming pool. His friend Hector lives 9 miles due east of the swimming pool. How far does Hector live from Ramon?

A 11 miles

B 13 miles

C 15 miles

D 17 miles

30. How far does Regina have to walk to school if she takes the nature trail?

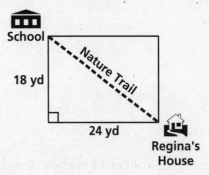

F 26 yd

G 28 yd

H 30 yd

J 32 yd

31. Which of the following three-dimensional figures has exactly one base?

   A cube

   B sphere

   C rectangular prism

   D rectangular pyramid

32. What three-dimensional figure is shown below?

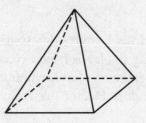

   F square pyramid

   G triangular prism

   H pentagonal prism

   J triangular pyramid

33. How many faces does a hexagonal prism have?

   A 5

   B 6

   C 7

   D 8

34. What is the volume of the box shown below?

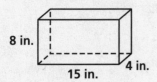

   F 120 in.^{3}

   G 240 in.^{3}

   H 360 in.^{3}

   J 480 in.^{3}

35. A large can of chicken noodle soup has a height of 5 inches and a diameter of 3 inches. What is the volume of this soup can to the nearest cubic inch? Use 3.14 as an approximation for π.

   A 35 in.^{3}

   B 37 in.^{3}

   C 45 in.^{3}

   D 47 in.^{3}

36. The side length of a cube is 5 centimeters. If the length of each side of the cube is increased by 2 centimeters, what is the difference between the volumes of the two cubes?

   F 24 cm^3

   G 125 cm^3

   H 218 cm^3

   J 342 cm^3

Name _____ Class _____ Date _____

Benchmark Test 5

1. What is the next term in the following sequence?

    2, 1.88, 1.76, 1.64, . . .

    A 1.42

    B 1.46

    C 1.52

    D 1.56

2. Which rule describes the sequence shown below?

    $8, 2, \frac{1}{2}, \frac{1}{8}, \ldots$

    F Start with 8 and multiply by $\frac{1}{4}$ repeatedly.

    G Start with 8 and divide by $\frac{1}{4}$ repeatedly.

    H Start with 8 and multiply by $\frac{1}{6}$ repeatedly.

    J Start with 8 and divide by $\frac{1}{6}$ repeatedly.

3. Look at the pattern shown below.

    How many black triangles will be in the fifteenth figure of the pattern?

    A 7

    B 8

    C 9

    D 10

4. What is the value of p in the table shown below?

x	y
1	16
3	48
6	p
9	144

    F 64

    G 80

    H 96

    J 128

5. The table below shows the prices of different types of bouquets at a florist shop.

    Bouquet Prices

Type	Number of Bouquets		
	1	2	3
Roses	$12.50	$25.00	$37.50
Violets	$5.25	$10.50	$15.75
Tulips	$4.75	$9.50	$14.25

    If the pattern shown in the table continues, how much will 5 bouquets of violets cost?

    A $23.75

    B $26.25

    C $45.00

    D $62.50

6. Each week Megan deposits money into her savings account. Her deposits are shown below.

Week	Deposit
1	$8.50
2	$10.75
3	$13.00
4	$15.25

If Megan continues this pattern, how much will she deposit in the tenth week?

F $24.25

G $26.50

H $28.75

J $31.00

7. Look at the function rule shown below.

$$y = 3x - 6$$

What is the value of y when $x = 3$?

A -3

B 0

C 3

D 9

8. Sam has $100 in his savings account. Each week he deposits $25. Which function rule can be used to determine the amount of money, m, in his account after w weeks?

F $m = \dfrac{25}{100}w$

G $m = 100w + 25$

H $m = 100 - 25w$

J $m = 100 + 25w$

9. Which rule describes the function represented in the table?

x	y
0	3
1	0
2	-3
3	-6

A $y = -3x + 3$

B $y = -x + 1$

C $y = x + 3$

D $y = -2x$

10. Jamie traveled from Ft. Lauderdale to Key West and stopped for lunch along the way. The graph below relates time and Jamie's distance from Ft. Lauderdale.

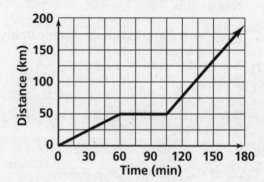

Based on the graph, how long did Jamie stop for lunch?

F 30 minutes

G 45 minutes

H 60 minutes

J 75 minutes

11. A runner jogs along a straight path at a constant speed, stops to rest for a while, and then starts to jog again. Which graph best represents the relationship between time and the runner's distance from a starting point?

A

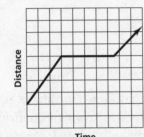

Time

B

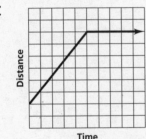

Time

C

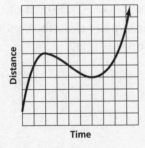

Time

D

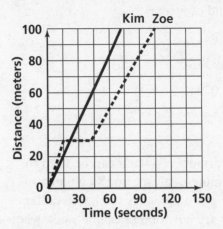

Time

12. Kim and Zoe swam in a 100 meter race. The graph shown below relates their time at their distance from the starting point.

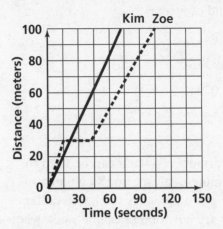

Kim Zoe

Which of the following *best* describes the race?

F Kim finished the race 30 seconds faster than Zoe.

G Zoe finished the race 30 seconds faster than Kim.

H Kim moved ahead of Zoe 45 seconds into the race.

J Zoe moved ahead of Kim 15 seconds into the race.

13. Raymond has $534 in a savings account that pays a simple annual interest rate of 3.5%. How much interest will the account earn in 5 years?

A $18.69   **C** $186.93

B $93.45   **D** $934.50

14. Michelle deposits $7,000 in a bank account at 4.5% interest compounded annually. How much will be in the account after 6 years?

F $8,890.00   **H** $16,803.20

G $9,115.82   **J** $43,890.00

15. Carlos borrowed $2,500 at an annual simple interest rate of 8.75%. If he makes no payments, how much money will he owe at the end of 3 years?

  A $656.25

  B $2,718.75

  C $3,020.83

  D $3,156.25

16. The formula $c = 0.02s$ can be used to determine a salesperson's commission, c, when given her sales total, s, in dollars. What are her total sales in a week when she earns a commission of $58?

  F $116

  G $290

  H $1,160

  J $2,900

17. Solve the equation $2x = 3y + 1$ for y.

  A $y = \dfrac{2x - 1}{3}$

  B $y = \dfrac{2x + 1}{3}$

  C $y = \dfrac{2}{3}x - 1$

  D $y = \dfrac{2}{3}x + 1$

18. A mechanic uses the formula $c = \$22.50h + p$ to calculate how much to charge a customer. In this formula, c is the amount the customer is charged, h is the number of hours the repair takes, and p is the cost of parts needed to make the repair. Solve this formula for h.

  F $h = \dfrac{c - p}{\$22.50}$

  G $h = \dfrac{c + p}{\$22.50}$

  H $h = \$22.50(c - p)$

  J $h = \$22.50(c + p)$

19. Which point on the coordinate graph below is located at $(-3, -2)$?

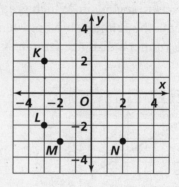

  A K

  B L

  C M

  D N

20. Point P has a negative x-coordinate and a positive y-coordinate. In which quadrant of the coordinate plane is point P located?

  F I

  G II

  H III

  J IV

21. A horizontal line passes through a point with coordinates $(-4, -2)$. Which of the following ordered pairs describes another point that lies on this line?

  A $(-4, 4)$

  B $(0, 0)$

  C $(2, -2)$

  D $(4, 2)$

22. Which graph represents the equation $x = -3$?

F

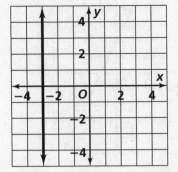

G

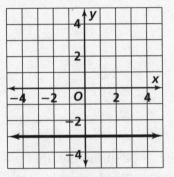

H

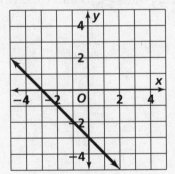

J

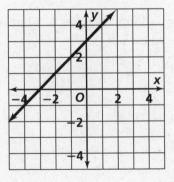

23. Which graph represents the linear equation that passes through the points listed in the table below?

x	y
−2	2
−1	1
0	0
1	−1

A

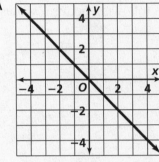

B

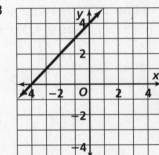

C

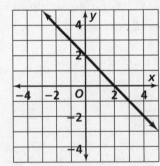

D

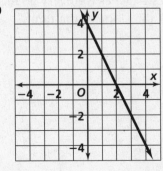

24. Which of the following lines, when graphed on a coordinate plane, will pass through the point with coordinates $(3, -4)$?

F $\ y = -x + 7$

G $\ y = -4x - 13$

H $\ y = 3x - 5$

J $\ y = 2x - 10$

25. A horizontal line contains the point $(5, 7)$. Which of the following points also lies on the line?

A $\ (-6, 7)$

B $\ (0, 5)$

C $\ (5, -2)$

D $\ (7, -3)$

26. Which of the following points does not lie on the graph of the equation $y = 5x - 3$?

F $\ (-2, 7)$

G $\ (1, 2)$

H $\ (0, -3)$

J $\ (3, 12)$

27. The point $(3, 4)$ lies on the graph of which of the following equations?

A $\ y = 3x - 4$

B $\ y = x + 4$

C $\ y = 4x - 6$

D $\ y = 2x - 2$

28. A ramp rises 2 inches for every 36 inches of run. What is the slope of the ramp?

F $\ \dfrac{1}{72}$

G $\ \dfrac{1}{18}$

H $\ 18$

J $\ 72$

29. What is the slope of the line graphed below?

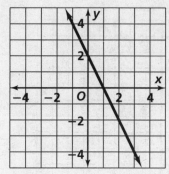

A $\ -2$

B $\ -\dfrac{1}{2}$

C $\ \dfrac{1}{2}$

D $\ 2$

30. What is the slope of the line that passes through the points $(4, 0)$ and $(0, -10)$?

F $\ -\dfrac{5}{2}$

G $\ -\dfrac{2}{5}$

H $\ \dfrac{2}{5}$

J $\ \dfrac{5}{2}$

31. For the equation $y = 2x^2 - 6$, what is the value of y when $x = 3$?

A $\ 0$

B $\ 6$

C $\ 12$

D $\ 18$

32. A construction worker drops a nail from a height of 200 feet. The equation $h = -16t^2 + 200$ can be used to find the nail's height, h, above the ground t seconds after it is dropped. What is the nail's height after 3 seconds?

F 3.5 feet

G 56 feet

H 144 feet

J 152 feet

33. Which equation is graphed below?

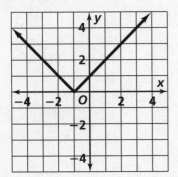

A $y = |x| - 1$

B $y = |x| + 1$

C $y = |x - 1|$

D $y = |x + 1|$

34. Point A is located at $(5, 3)$. If it is translated up 5 units and left 4 units, what are the coordinates of the image A'?

F $(0, -1)$

G $(0, 7)$

H $(1, 8)$

J $(10, 7)$

35. Which figure on the graph shown below is a translation of $\triangle RST$?

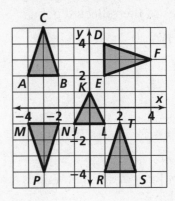

A $\triangle ABC$

B $\triangle DEF$

C $\triangle JKL$

D $\triangle MNP$

36. Figure $ABCD$ is translated to produce figure $A'B'C'D'$. Which rule describes the translation of figure $ABCD$?

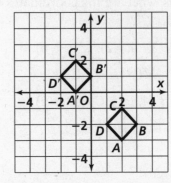

F $(x, y) \rightarrow (x + 3, y - 3)$

G $(x, y) \rightarrow (x - 3, y - 3)$

H $(x, y) \rightarrow (x + 3, y + 3)$

J $(x, y) \rightarrow (x - 3, y + 3)$

37. If the point with coordinates $(6, -7)$ is reflected over the y-axis, what are the coordinates of the reflected point?

A $(-6, -7)$

B $(-6, 7)$

C $(6, -7)$

D $(6, 7)$

38. How many lines of symmetry does a regular pentagon have?

F 0

G 1

H 5

J 10

39. The graph of $\triangle ABC$ has vertices at $A(6, 3)$, $B(4, 2)$, and $C(-2, 6)$. If $\triangle ABC$ is reflected over the x-axis, what are the coordinates of its image $\triangle A'B'C'$?

A $A'(-6, 3), B'(-4, -2), C'(-2, 6)$

B $A'(-6, -3), B'(-4, -2), C'(2, -6)$

C $A'(6, -3), B'(4, -2), C'(-2, -6)$

D $A'(6, 3), B'(4, -2), C'(-2, 6)$

STOP

Quarter 1 Test

Chapters 1–3

Form A

1. Use front-end estimation to estimate the sum to the nearest whole number.

   $3.59 + 44.603 + 16.24$

2. At the Colorado ski meet, the French Canadian skier jumped 89.5234 meters. The American skier jumped 90.06 meters. How much farther did the American skier jump than the Canadian skier?

3. Jennifer needed material for her 4-H project. She bought 3.25 yards of material for $8.82 per yard. What was the total cost of the material? Round to the nearest cent.

4. Convert.

   $25 \text{ m} = \underline{\hspace{2cm}} \text{cm}$

5. Find $|-16|$.

6. Mary has a score of 7 in a game. If she loses 10 points, what is her new score?

7. A submarine descends from the surface (0 meters) to -150 meters in 3 minutes. What was the change in depth per minute?

8. Order from least to greatest.

   $\frac{1}{4}, 0.3, -\frac{7}{8}, -2$

9. Simplify. $3^3 \times (7 - 2)^2$

10. Write 7,000,000,000 in scientific notation.

11. Write a number less than 100 that is divisible by 2, 5, and 9.

12. Write the fraction $\frac{42}{49}$ in simplest form.

13. Order from least to greatest.

    $\frac{9}{10}, \frac{8}{11}, \frac{7}{9}$

14. Write $\frac{15}{7}$ as a mixed number.

15. At the local drugstore, it costs $.35 to get a negative of a picture developed. If Lauren spent $3.85 getting negatives developed, how many pictures did she get?

16. Find the GCF of this pair of numbers.

    77 and 154

17. Casey got 32 out of 40 questions correct on her social studies test. Last week she got 24 out of 30 questions correct. Which score was better? Explain.

18. An athlete runs $1\frac{3}{4}$ mi in the morning and $2\frac{1}{8}$ mi in the evening. Estimate to the nearest mile the total number of miles the athlete runs in one day.

19. A juice drink is made of $\frac{1}{3}$ apple juice, $\frac{2}{5}$ grape juice, and the rest, water. What fraction of the drink is made of juice?

20. Find the difference.

$13\frac{1}{6} - 5\frac{5}{6}$

21. Find the product.

$2\frac{1}{10} \times 3\frac{2}{3}$

22. Find the quotient.

$4\frac{1}{6} \div 3\frac{1}{2}$

23. Complete.

69 ft = _____ yd

24. Choose the more precise measurement.

3 g or 16.4 g

25. Write in standard form.

3.6×10^4

26. Mike ran $2\frac{2}{3}$ mi. Joe ran $1\frac{1}{6}$ mi. How much farther did Mike run than Joe?

27. You have 20 beads to make a bracelet. Each bead is $\frac{3}{8}$ in. long. How long will the bracelet be?

28. How many $\frac{2}{3}$-oz slices of cheese are in a 16-oz package?

29. You stand on a scale holding your cat. The scale reads 130 lb 12 oz. Alone, you weigh $120\frac{1}{2}$ lb. How much does your cat weigh?

30. A hiker's backpack weighs 18 lb fully packed. The backpack itself weighs 2 lb 4 oz. What is the weight of the backpack's contents?

31. Find the sum. Round your answer to the most appropriate degree of precision.

8.41 in. + 6.3 in.

32. Use compatible numbers to estimate the quotient.

$16\frac{1}{3} \div 3\frac{7}{8}$

Quarter 1 Test
Form B
Chapters 1–3

1. Use front-end estimation to estimate the sum to the nearest whole number.

   13.40 + 36.63 + 125.042

2. At the school swim meet, Tonya swam her race in 34.56 seconds, and Maria swam her race in 33.23 seconds. How much faster did Maria swim her race than Tonya?

3. Mr. Jung needs 4 lb of lunchmeat for a luncheon he is planning. If the lunchmeat costs $4.79 per pound, how much will the meat for the lunch cost?

4. Convert.

   320 mL = _____ L

5. Find $|-21|$.

6. Augusta had 60 points in a game. She lost a certain number of points, which resulted in a new score of −10. How many points did she lose?

7. At South Grove High School, the average change in enrollment was −65 students per year during the last 5 years. What was the total change in enrollment during that time period?

8. Order from least to greatest.

   $\frac{2}{3}, -\frac{1}{2}, -2, 0.5$

9. Simplify. $4^3 + 18 \div 3$

10. Write 596,000 in scientific notation.

11. Write a number less than 100 that is divisible by 3, 4, and 7.

12. Write the fraction $\frac{35}{60}$ in simplest form.

13. Order from least to greatest.

    $\frac{5}{6}, \frac{7}{4}, \frac{11}{12}$

14. Write $\frac{17}{6}$ as a mixed number.

15. Tina spent $3.00 on raffle tickets. They cost $0.75 each. How many did she get?

16. Find the GCF of this pair of numbers.

    84 and 14

17. During a soccer game, Erin scored 5 out of 8 goals attempted. Lauren scored 7 out of 10 goals attempted. Find each player's percentage of successful shots. Compare to determine who was the most successful.

18. You need $4\frac{1}{4}$ yd of cloth for your costume and $4\frac{5}{8}$ yd of cloth for your sister's costume. Estimate to the nearest yard the total yardage of cloth that you need.

19. John practices playing his trumpet for $\frac{3}{8}$ of an hour before school and $\frac{3}{4}$ of an hour after school. How long does John practice on his trumpet on school days?

20. Find the sum.

$12\frac{1}{8} + 5\frac{5}{6}$

21. Find the product.

$6\frac{1}{4} \times 1\frac{1}{5}$

22. Find the quotient.

$3\frac{3}{10} \div 1\frac{1}{2}$

23. Complete.

72 in. = _____ ft

24. Choose the more precise measurement.

4 mL or 24.2 mL

25. Write in standard form.

4.1×10^3

26. Julie bought $3\frac{3}{4}$ yd of silk cord. She used $\frac{5}{8}$ yd for a bag drawstring. How much cord does she have left?

27. On the test, $\frac{3}{8}$ of the students in the class made an A. How many of the 24 students made an A?

28. How many $1\frac{1}{2}$ in.-wide stamps will fit in a row across a 20 in.-wide page?

29. In 1993 a Cuban man set the world record in the outdoor high jump by jumping $96\frac{1}{2}$ in. How many feet high is this?

30. Eva can swim 3000 meters in 1 h 45 min. Jill swims it in $1\frac{5}{8}$ h. Who is the faster swimmer?

31. Find the sum. Round your answer to the most appropriate degree of precision.

9.46 g + 10.3 g

32. Use compatible numbers to estimate the quotient.

$11\frac{3}{4} \div 1\frac{3}{4}$

Quarter 1 Test · · · · · · · · · · · · · · · · · · · Form D

Chapters 1–3

1. Estimate the sum.

   $3.59 + 16.24$

2. Simplify.

   $6.2 - 4.38$

3. Jennifer needed material for her 4-H project. She bought 3.25 yards of material for $8.82 per yard. What was the total cost of the material? Round to the nearest cent.

4. Convert.

   $25 \text{ m} = \underline{\hspace{1cm}} \text{cm}$

5. Find $|-16|$.

6. Simplify.

   $17 + (-10)$

7. Simplify.

   $6 - (-9)$

8. Simplify.

   $3^3 \times (7 - 2)^2$

9. Write 7,000,000,000 in scientific notation.

10. Write the fraction $\frac{42}{49}$ in simplest form.

11. Order from least to greatest.

    $\frac{3}{4}, \frac{2}{3}, \frac{1}{6}$

12. Write $\frac{15}{7}$ as a mixed number.

13. At the local drugstore, it costs $.35 to get a negative of a picture developed. If Lauren spent $3.85 getting negatives developed, how many pictures did she get?

14. Find the GCF of this pair of numbers.

    77 and 154

15. Write the fraction as a decimal.

$\frac{5}{8}$

16. An athlete runs $1\frac{3}{4}$ mi in the morning and $2\frac{1}{8}$ mi in the evening. Estimate to the nearest mile the total number of miles the athlete runs in one day.

17. A juice drink is made of $\frac{1}{3}$ apple juice, $\frac{2}{5}$ grape juice, and the rest, water. What fraction of the drink is made of juice?

18. Find the difference.

$13\frac{1}{6} - 5\frac{5}{6}$

19. Complete.

69 ft = _____ yd

20. Choose the more precise measurement.

3 g or 16.4 g

21. Write in standard form.

3.6×10^4

22. You have 20 beads to make a bracelet. Each bead is $\frac{3}{8}$ in. long. How long will the bracelet be?

23. How many $\frac{2}{3}$-oz slices of cheese are in a 16-oz package?

24. Find the difference.

130 lb $- 120\frac{1}{2}$ lb

Quarter 1 Test
Chapters 1–3

Form E

1. Estimate the sum.

   $13.40 + 36.63$

2. Simplify.

   $7.4 - 3.56$

3. Mr. Jung needs 4 lbs of lunchmeat for a luncheon he is planning. If the lunchmeat costs $4.79 per pound, how much will the meat for the lunch cost?

4. Convert.

   $320 \text{ mL} = \underline{\hspace{2cm}} \text{L}$

5. Find $|-21|$.

6. Simplify.

   $(-10) + 4$

7. Simplify.

   $(-14) - 8$

8. Simplify.

   $4^3 + 18 \div 3$

9. Write 596,000 in scientific notation.

10. Write the fraction $\frac{35}{60}$ in simplest form.

11. Place in order from least to greatest.

    $\frac{5}{6}, \frac{7}{4}, \frac{11}{12}$

12. Write $\frac{17}{6}$ as a mixed number.

13. Tina spent $3.00 on raffle tickets. They cost $0.75 each. How many did she get?

14. Find the GCF of this pair of numbers.

84 and 14

15. Write the fraction as a decimal.

$\frac{7}{8}$

16. You need $4\frac{1}{4}$ yd of cloth for your costume and $4\frac{5}{8}$ yd of cloth for your sister's costume. Estimate to the nearest yard the total yardage of cloth that you need for both costumes.

17. John practices playing his trumpet for $\frac{3}{8}$ of an hour before school and $\frac{3}{4}$ of an hour after school. How long does John practice on his trumpet on school days?

18. Find the sum.

$12\frac{1}{8} + 5\frac{5}{6}$

19. Complete.

72 in. = _____ ft

20. Choose the more precise measurement.

4 mL or 24.2 mL

21. Write in standard form.

4.1×10^3

22. How many $1\frac{1}{2}$-in.-wide stamps will fit in a row across a 20-in.-wide page?

23. On the test, $\frac{3}{8}$ of the students in the class made an A. How many of the 24 students made an A?

24. Find the sum.

9.46 g + 10.3 g

Quarter 2 Test

Form A

Chapters 4–6

For Exercises 1–3, solve each equation.

1. $d + 14 = 27$

2. $\frac{p}{7} = 15$

3. $\frac{x}{4} + 3 = -7$

4. You swam a race in 59.60 seconds. This is 0.06 seconds faster than your opponent's time. Write and solve an equation to find your opponent's time.

5. Rashaan earned $60 mowing lawns this weekend. He charges $15 per lawn. Write and solve an equation to find the number of lawns he mowed.

6. Explain how to solve the equation $3t + 11 = -10$.

7. Josh bought packs of baseball cards for $.79 each and a card container for $3.98. The total cost of Josh's purchases was $7.93. Write an equation to determine how many packs of cards Josh bought.

8. Write a word phrase for the algebraic expression $\frac{x}{4} + 5$.

9. Write the inequality for the graph.

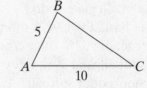

For Exercises 10 and 11, solve each inequality.

10. $x - 0.234 \geq 7.021$

11. $\frac{m}{-6} < 5$

12. Write the ratio in 2 different ways.

    24 baseballs to 18 baseball bats

13. Express as a unit rate.

    144 attempted passes for 36 completions

14. Kevin scored 80 points in 5 basketball games. At this rate, how many points will he score in 16 games?

15. An adult African male elephant weighs about 12,000 pounds and has tusks about 8 feet long. An adult Indian male elephant weighs about 8,000 pounds and has tusks about 5 feet long. Are the weight-to-tusk-length ratios of African and Indian male elephants equivalent? Explain.

16. $\triangle ABC \sim \triangle DEF$. Find x.

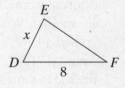

17. When a maple tree's shadow is 9 feet long, a redwood tree's shadow is 22.5 feet long. If the maple tree is 30 feet high, how high is the redwood?

18. What is the scale of a map if a 20-mile highway is shown as 4 inches long?

19. Write 0.023 as a percent.

20. Write 40% as a decimal.

21. Write $\frac{7}{5}$ as a percent.

22. Write 47% as a fraction.

23. What percent of 72 is 24?

24. ABC Industries employs 294 workers who live within 5 miles of their factory. If 30% of all employees live within 5 miles of the factory, what is the total number of employees at ABC Industries?

25. An NCAA survey of 802 four-year colleges offering women's intercollegiate sports shows that 96% offer basketball, 91% offer volleyball, 89% offer tennis, 82% offer cross country, 71% offer softball, and 69% offer track. How many schools offer softball?

26. You buy a pair of running shoes for a discount of 12% from the regular selling price of $69.95. How much do the shoes cost? Round to the nearest cent.

27. The wholesale price for an item that regularly sells for $22.23 is $19.50. What is the percentage markup for this item?

28. Solve the proportion. $\frac{4}{7} = \frac{x}{49}$

29. The number of students that signed up for a class was 64. Then a flyer went out and the number enrolled increased by 25%. How many were now enrolled?

30. Define the term *scale drawing* in your own words.

31. Your parents just bought a new television and stereo system for $2,250. They made a down payment of $750 and will pay the rest of the cost in equal monthly payments over the next year. Write and solve an equation for the amount of each payment.

32. Mario works as a salesperson. He earns $400 per week plus a 4% commission on all sales. If he sells $1,650 worth of goods in one week, what will his total earnings that week be?

Quarter 2 Test
Chapters 4–6

Form B

For Exercises 1–3, solve each equation.

1. $e - 11 = 2.9$

2. $\frac{t}{2} = 8.6$

3. $3x + 11 = 10$

4. You jumped 16.5 feet in a track and field competition. This is 2 feet farther than your opponent's jump. Write and solve an equation to find your opponent's jump length.

5. Twyla earned $30 baby-sitting last week. She charges $5 per hour. Write and solve an equation to find the number of hours she baby-sat.

6. Explain how to solve the equation $\frac{j}{4} + 3 = -7$.

7. Mrs. Baker purchased a number of juice boxes at a cost of $0.30 each and a loaf of bread that cost $1.19. The total cost of her purchases was $2.99. Write an equation to determine the number of juice boxes Mrs. Baker purchased.

8. Write a word phrase for the algebraic expression $2x - 5$.

9. Write an inequality for this graph.

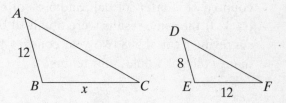

For Exercises 10 and 11, solve each inequality.

10. $1.4 + x \le 7$

11. $\frac{m}{10} < -4$

12. Write the ratio in 2 different ways.

    16 apples to 14 pears

13. Express as a unit rate.

    112 pitches for 28 foul balls

14. Harold has scored 16 goals in 5 soccer games. At this rate, how many goals will he score in 15 games?

15. An adult African male elephant is about 11 feet tall and weighs about 12,000 pounds. An adult African female elephant is about 9 feet tall and weighs about 9,000 pounds. Are the weight-to-height ratios of male and female African elephants equivalent? Explain.

16. $\triangle ABC \sim \triangle DEF$. Find x.

17. When a flagpole's shadow is 10 feet long, the shadow of a building is 30 feet long. If the flagpole is 75 feet tall, how tall is the building?

18. What is the scale of a map if a 15-mile highway is shown as 3 inches long?

19. Write 0.058 as a percent.

20. Write 72% as a decimal.

21. Write $\frac{9}{8}$ as a percent.

22. Write 35% as a fraction.

23. What percent of 96 is 24?

24. The price of an item in a store is 20% of its original price. It is now selling for $80. How much did the item cost originally?

25. An NCAA survey of 802 four-year colleges offering women's intercollegiate sports shows that 96% offer basketball, 91% offer volleyball, 89% offer tennis, 82% offer cross country, 71% offer softball, and 69% offer track. If the same results were obtained by surveying a set of 508 two-year colleges, how many colleges would offer tennis?

26. Which costs less, a pair of $95 skis on sale for 10% off, or a $120 pair at 25% off?

27. Chelsea increased her bowling score from 200 to 250. Find the percent increase.

28. Solve the proportion. $\frac{5}{8} = \frac{x}{72}$

29. After Todd received a 3% salary increase, his new yearly salary was $25,750. What was his yearly salary before the increase?

30. Define the term *scale* in your own words.

31. Your parents just bought a new computer for $2,100. They made a down payment of $300 and will pay the rest of the cost in equal monthly payments over the next two years. Write and solve an equation for the amount of each payment.

32. Mario works as a salesperson. He earns $350 per week plus a 6% commission on all sales. If he sells $1,540 worth of goods in one week, what will his total earnings that week be?

Quarter 2 Test

Form D

Chapters 4–6

1. Solve. $d + 14 = 27$

2. Rashaan earned \$60 mowing lawns this weekend. He charges \$15 per lawn. Write and solve an equation for the number of lawns he mowed.

3. Explain how to solve the equation $3t + 11 = -10$.

4. Josh bought packs of baseball cards for \$.79 each and a card container for \$3.98. The total cost of Josh's purchases was \$7.93. Write an equation to determine how many packs of cards Josh bought.

5. Write an algebraic expression for this phrase:

the price of a pizza m divided among 4 friends

6. Write an inequality for this graph.

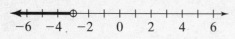

For Exercises 7 and 8, solve each inequality.

7. $x - 0.23 \geq 7.02$

8. $\dfrac{m}{-6} < 5$

9. Write this ratio in 2 different ways.

24 baseballs to 18 baseball bats

10. Express as a unit rate:

144 attempted passes for 36 completions

11. Kevin scored 80 points in 5 basketball games. At this rate, how many points will he score in 16 games?

12. Do these ratios form a proportion?

$\dfrac{8}{12}$ and $\dfrac{5}{8}$

13. $\triangle ABC \sim \triangle DEF$. Find x.

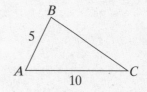
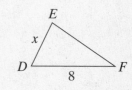

14. When a maple tree's shadow is 9 feet long, a redwood tree's shadow is 22.5 feet long. If the maple tree is 30 feet high, how high is the redwood?

15. What is the scale of a map if a 20-mile highway is shown as 4 inches long?

16. Write 0.023 as a percent.

17. Write 40% as a decimal.

18. Write $\frac{7}{5}$ as a percent.

19. Write 47% as a fraction.

20. What percent of 72 is 24?

21. ABC Industries employs 294 workers who live within 5 miles of their factory. This is 30% of their total employees. What is their total employee count?

22. You buy a pair of running shoes for a discount of 12% from the regular selling price of $69.95. How much do the shoes cost? Round to the nearest cent.

23. Find the percent of markup.

$19 marked up to $22

24. Find the percent of increase.

64 to 80

25. Find the commission on a $1,650 sale with a commission rate of 4%.

Quarter 2 Test
Form E
Chapters 4–6

1. Solve.

   $e - 11 = 2.9$

2. Twyla earned $30 babysitting last week. She charges $5 per hour. Write and solve an equation for how many hours she worked.

3. Explain how to solve the equation $\frac{m}{4} + 3 = -7$.

4. Mrs. Baker purchased a number of juice boxes at a cost of $0.30 each and a loaf of bread that cost $1.19. The total cost of her purchases was $2.99. Write an equation to find how many juice boxes Mrs. Baker purchased.

5. Write an algebraic expression for this phrase:

   10 pages more than *x* pages

6. Write an inequality for this graph.

For Exercises 7 and 8, solve each inequality.

7. $1.4 + x \leq 7$

8. $\frac{m}{10} < -4$

9. Write this ratio in 2 different ways.

   16 apples to 14 pears

10. Express as a unit rate:

    112 pitches for 28 foul balls

11. Harold has scored 16 goals in 5 soccer games. At this rate, how many goals will he score in 15 games?

12. Do these ratios form a proportion?

    $\frac{9}{12}$ and $\frac{3}{4}$

13. $\triangle ABC \sim \triangle DEF$. Find *x*.

    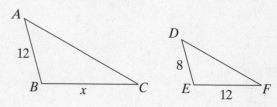

14. When a flagpole's shadow is 10 feet long, the shadow of a building is 30 feet long. If the flagpole is 75 feet tall, how tall is the building?

21. The price of an item in a store is 20% of its original price. It is now selling for $80. How much was it originally?

15. What is the scale of a map if a 15-mile highway is shown as 3 inches long?

22. Which costs less, a pair of $95 skis on sale for 10% off, or a $120 pair at 25% off?

23. Find the percent of markup.

$25 marked up to $33

16. Write 0.058 as a percent.

17. Write 72% as a decimal.

24. Find the percent of increase.

200 to 250

18. Write $\frac{9}{8}$ as a percent.

25. Find the commission on a $1,540 sale with a commission rate of 6%.

19. Write 35% as a fraction.

20. What percent of 96 is 24?

Quarter 3 Test

Form A

Chapters 7–9

1. Use a straightedge to draw $\overleftrightarrow{AB}$.

2. Classify the angle below.

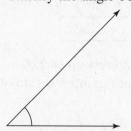

3. The complement of an angle is 29°. What is the measure of the angle?

4. $\overline{JK}$ bisects $\overline{LM}$ at point *D*. What can you say about *D*?

5. Classify the three triangles having the following sets of angles: (1) 30°, 60°, 90°; (2) 55°, 30°, 95°; (3) 55°, 55°, 70°.

6. The measures of two angles of a triangle are 68° and 54°. Find the measure of the third angle.

7. Name a polygon with six sides.

8. Use the triangles below.

    a. $\triangle ABC \cong \triangle$ _____

    b. $\angle BCA \cong \angle$ _____

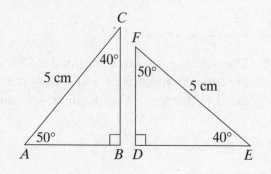

9. Name a diameter for circle *C* below.

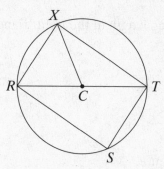

10. The number of hours a student spends doing homework in a month is represented by the circle graph below. What percent of these hours is spent on math and history combined? Round to the nearest tenth.

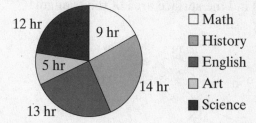

11. Find the area.

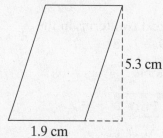

12. Find the area.

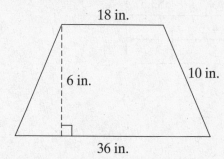

13. Simplify. $\sqrt{196}$

14. Find the missing length in the right triangle.

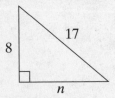

15. Identify the figure.

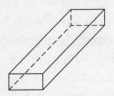

16. Find the surface area of the triangular prism.

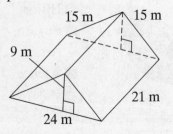

17. What are the next two terms in the sequence $-3, 9, -27, 81, \ldots$?

18. Complete the table.

Apples (lb)	Price
1	$1.19
2	$2.38
3	$3.57
4	
5	

19. Write a function rule for the numbers in the table.

n	4	5	6	7
f(n)	16	25	36	49

20. What is the simple interest on $4,225 principal borrowed at the interest rate of 7.25% for 1 year?

21. Solve for a in the equation $\frac{1}{4}a - b = c$.

22. Find the area of the shaded figure. The area of each square is 1 cm^2.

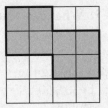

23. Find the volume of a rectangular prism that is 8 inches long, 6 inches wide, and 5 inches high.

24. A right triangle has one angle that measures 42°. What are the measures of the other two angles? Show your work.

25. Classify the quadrilateral below as many ways as you can.

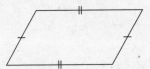

26. The diameter of a circular pond is 27 feet. Find the circumference and area of the pond to the nearest tenth. Show your work.

Quarter 3 Test

Form B

Chapters 7–9

1. Use a straightedge to draw $\overrightarrow{XY}$.

2. Classify the angle below.

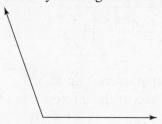

3. The supplement of an angle is 29°. What is the measure of the angle?

4. Name the three segment bisectors of $\overline{HF}$.

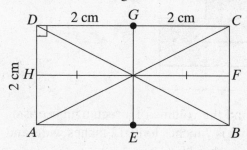

5. Classify the three triangles having the following lengths of sides.

    a. 12, 5, 24

    b. 7, 7, 7

    c. 15, 20, 15

6. The measures of two angles of a triangle are 42° and 52°. Find the measure of the third angle.

7. Name a polygon with eight sides.

8. Use the triangles below. $\triangle MNO \cong \triangle PQR$.
    a. $\angle N \cong \angle$ _____   b. $\angle O \cong \angle$ _____

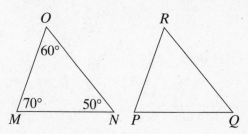

9. Name a chord for circle C below.

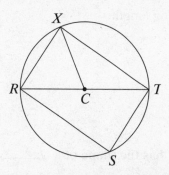

10. The circle graph below represents a family's monthly budget. If the total monthly budget is $1,700, how much money is spent on housing?

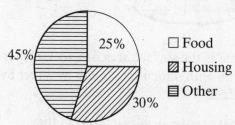

11. Find the area of this triangle.

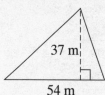

12. Find the area.

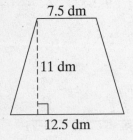

7.5 dm

11 dm

12.5 dm

13. Simplify. $\sqrt{144}$

14. Find the missing length.

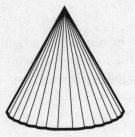

x 25

7

15. This party hat has the shape of a _____.

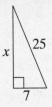

16. What is the surface area of a rectangular prism with dimensions 3 feet by 2 feet by 12 feet?

17. What are the next two terms in the sequence 100, 50, 25, . . . ?

18. Complete the table.

Bagels (dozen)	Price
1	$4.99
2	$9.98
3	$14.97
4	
5	

19. Write a function rule for the numbers in the table.

n	2	3	4	5
$f(n)$	8	27	64	125

20. What is the simple interest on $5,820 principal borrowed at the interest rate of 9.5% for 1 year?

21. Solve for r in the equation $A = 2\pi r$.

22. Find the area of the shaded figure. The area of each square is 2 cm^2.

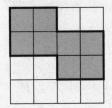

23. Find the volume of a rectangular prism that is 7 inches long, 12 inches wide, and 15 inches high.

24. An isosceles triangle has one obtuse angle that measures 102°. What are the measures of the other two angles? Show your work.

25. Classify this quadrilateral as many ways as you can.

26. A farmer makes a large crop circle in his field. The diameter of the crop circle is 64 feet. Find the circumference and area of the crop circle to the nearest tenth. Show your work.

Quarter 3 Test

Form D

Chapters 7–9

1. Use a straightedge to draw $\overleftrightarrow{AB}$.

2. Classify the angle below.

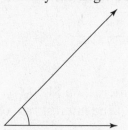

3. The complement of an angle is 30°. What is the measure of the angle?

4. $\overline{JK}$ bisects $\overline{LM}$ at point D. What can you say about D?

5. Classify a triangle having the following set of angles: 30°, 60°, 90°.

6. The measures of two angles of a triangle are 68° and 54°. Find the measure of the third angle.

7. Name a polygon with six sides.

8. Use the triangles below.

   a. $\triangle ABC \cong \triangle$ _____

   b. $\angle BCA \cong \angle$ _____

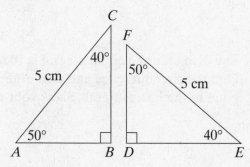

9. Name a diameter for circle C below.

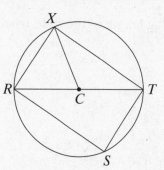

10. The number of hours a student spends doing homework in a month is represented by the circle graph below. What percent of these hours is spent on math? Round to the nearest tenth.

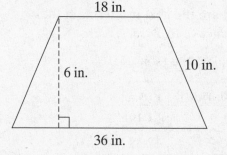

11. Find the area:

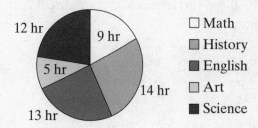

12. Simplify. $\sqrt{100}$

13. Find the missing length in the right triangle.

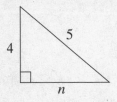

14. Identify the figure.

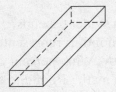

15. Find the surface area of the triangular prism.

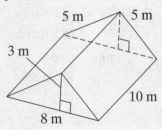

16. What are the next two terms in the sequence 8, 16, 24, 32, . . . ?

17. Complete the table.

Apples (lb)	Price
1	$1.19
2	$2.38
3	$3.57
4	
5	

18. Write a function rule for the numbers in the table.

n	4	5	6	7
f(n)	13	14	15	16

19. What is the simple interest on $1,500 principal borrowed at the interest rate of 5% for 1 year?

20. Solve for a in the equation $\frac{1}{4}a - b = c$.

21. Find the area of the shaded figure. The area of each square is 1 cm^2.

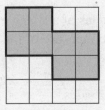

22. Find the volume of a rectangular prism that is 8 inches long, 6 inches wide, and 5 inches high.

23. The diameter of a circular pond is 10 feet. Find the circumference and area of the pond to the nearest tenth. Show your work.

Quarter 3 Test

Chapters 7–9

Form E

1. Use a straightedge to draw $\overrightarrow{XY}$.

2. Classify the angle below.

3. The supplement of an angle is 30°. What is the measure of the angle?

4. Name one segment bisector of $\overline{HF}$.

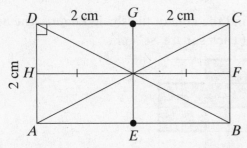

5. Classify the triangle having the side lengths 15, 22, 15.

6. The measures of two angles of a triangle are 42° and 52°. Find the measure of the third angle.

7. Name a polygon with eight sides.

8. Use the triangles below. $\triangle MNO \cong \triangle PQR$.
   a. $\angle N \cong \angle$ _____ b. $\angle O \cong \angle$ _____

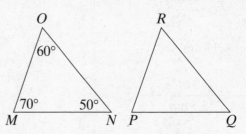

9. Name a chord for circle C below.

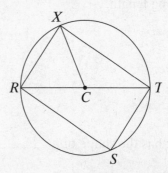

10. The circle graph below represents a family's monthly budget. If the total monthly budget is $1,700, how much money is spent on housing?

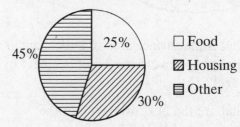

11. Find the area of this triangle.

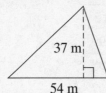

12. Find the area.

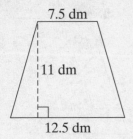

7.5 dm

11 dm

12.5 dm

13. Simplify. $\sqrt{81}$

14. Find the missing length.

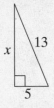

x 13

5

15. This party hat has the shape of a _____.

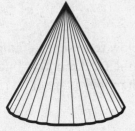

16. What is the surface area of a rectangular prism with dimensions 3 feet by 2 feet by 12 feet?

17. What are the next two terms in the sequence 1, 4, 9, 16, 25, . . . ?

18. Complete the table.

Bagels (dozen)	Price
1	$4.99
2	$9.98
3	$14.97
4	
5	

19. Write a function rule for the numbers in the table.

n	2	3	4	5
$f(n)$	8	12	16	20

20. What is the simple interest on $1,200 principal borrowed at the interest rate of 4% for 1 year?

21. Solve for r in the equation $A = 2\pi r$.

22. Find the area of the shaded figure. The area of each square is 2 cm^2.

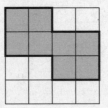

23. Find the volume of a rectangular prism that is 7 inches long, 10 inches wide, and 15 inches high.

24. A farmer makes a large crop circle in his field. The diameter of the crop circle is 60 feet. Find the circumference and area of the crop circle to the nearest tenth. Show your work.

Quarter 4 Test

Form A

Chapters 10–12

1. In which quadrant is the point with coordinates $(14, -13)$ located?

2. Write an ordered pair that is a solution of the equation $3x + 2y = -11$. Make sure that the x and y values in the ordered pair are integers less than 10 and greater than -10.

3. Without plotting points, explain which of these two equations is shown in the graph. $y = 2x - 1, y = -2x + 1$.

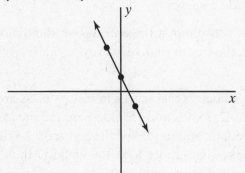

4. Which point is at $(1, -2)$?

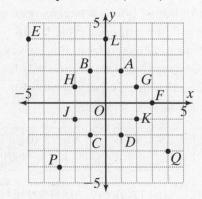

5. Write the absolute value equation shown by the graph below.

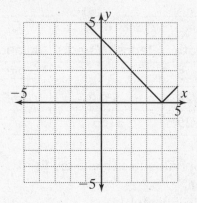

6. Point B below is translated up 4 units. What are its new coordinates?

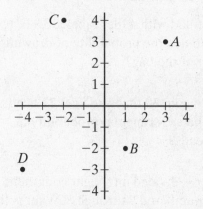

7. Write the coordinates of the ordered pair $(3, -2)$ after the translation $(x, y) \rightarrow (x + 2, y - 3)$.

8. Draw a line of symmetry on this figure.

9. The figure on the left was rotated clockwise to the position shown on the right. How much was it rotated?

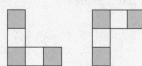

10. In the spreadsheet below, what balance belongs in cell C3?

	A	B	C
	Date	Deposit/Checks	Balance
1	6/25		$255
2	6/28	–$310	–$55
3	6/29	$165	

11. Use a proportion to estimate the fish population.
Total fish counted: 1,151
Tagged fish counted: 99
Total tagged fish: 436

12. A bag is filled with 4 tiles labeled D, E, F, and G. What is the probability of drawing a *vowel* out of the bag?

13. You toss a coin 30 times and get 12 heads. What is the experimental probability of getting heads?

14. A spinner is divided into eight congruent sections, numbered 1 through 8. What is the probability of spinning two 1s in a row?

15. How many ways can 4 books be placed on a shelf from a selection of 7 possible books?

16. Calculate 3!.

17. Look at the stem-and-leaf plot below. How many students earned a score of 84?

Math Test Scores

```
9 | 2
8 | 4 4 5 6
7 | 2 2 5 5 8
6 | 0 1 2 5
```
Key: 6 | 2 means 62.

18. A cafe offers a choice of 5 different sandwiches, 4 different side dishes, and 6 different drinks for lunch. How many different lunches can be selected?

19. A deli restaurant offers only one type of bagel, but customers can choose any 3 of 6 available toppings. How many different combinations of 3 toppings are there?

20. Which sample is more likely to be random? Explain.

  a. You walk through the halls of a school to do a survey.

  b. You stand at the entrance of the biology classroom to do a survey.

21. A student's test scores in history class are 92, 82, 75, 91, and 75. Compare the mean, median, and mode for the test scores. Which makes the grades look the highest? the lowest? Show your work and explain.

22. A survey is conducted among a group of seventh-grade students to determine the average number of books a twelve-year-old reads yearly. The frequency table below shows the data collected from this survey. Identify two possible sizes of intervals for representing this data. Give a reason for each size of interval selected.

Number	1	2	3	4	5	6	7	8	9	10	11	12
Tally			II	IIII		II	₪I		III		₪I	IIII

Number	13	14	15	16	17	18	19	20	21	22	23	24
Tally		₪IIII	II		I	IIII	II	₪IIII		II		₪I

Quarter 4 Test

Form B

Chapters 10–12

1. In which quadrant is the point with coordinates $(-12, -11)$ located?

2. Determine if the ordered pair $(-4, 2)$ is a solution of $4x - 3y = -10$.

3. Without plotting points, explain which of these two equations is shown in the graph. $y = 6x - 1, y = -5x - 1$.

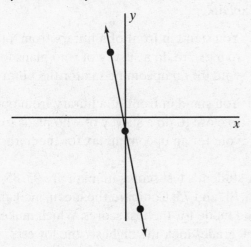

4. Which point is at $(-2, 4)$?

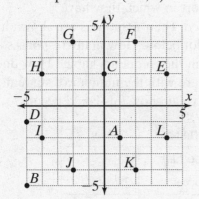

5. Graph $y = -x^2 + 4$ using integer values from -3 to 3.

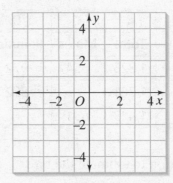

6. Point D below is translated down 2 units and to the right 5 units. What are its new coordinates?

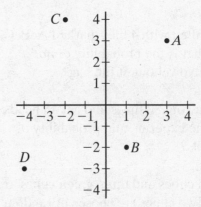

7. Write the coordinates of the ordered pair $(8, 3)$ after the translation of left 4 down 6.

8. Draw a line of symmetry on the figure.

9. The figure on the left was rotated clockwise to the position shown on the right. How much was it rotated?

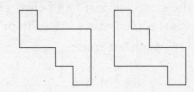

10. What number goes in cell D4 in the spreadsheet below?

	A	B	C	D
1	High School	Total	Males	Females
2	Southwest	1,826	854	972
3	Marshall	1,781		852
4	Washburn	1,423	631	

11. Use a proportion to estimate the bird population.
Total birds counted: 436
Banded birds counted: 50
Total banded birds: 70

12. A bag is filled with 4 tiles marked A, B, C, and D. What is the probability of *not* drawing a vowel out of the bag?

13. You toss a coin 80 times and get 45 heads. What is the experimental probability of getting tails?

14. Seven red cubes and three green cubes are in a bag. Two cubes are chosen at random without replacement. Find P(red, then green).

15. Five friends are standing side by side to get their pictures taken. In how many different orders can they stand?

16. Calculate 6!.

17. Look at the stem-and-leaf plot below. How many students earned scores in the 70s or 80s?

Math Test Scores
```
9 | 2
8 | 4 4 5 6
7 | 2 2 5 5 8
6 | 0 1 2 5
```
Key: 7 | 5 means 75.

18. There are 5 students running for class president and 6 running for class vice president. How many different ways can a voter select one candidate for each office?

19. A yogurt shop offers sundaes made from a choice of 4 flavors of yogurt, 6 different toppings, and 3 different types of nuts. Use the counting principle to find the number of different sundaes.

20. Which sample is more likely to be random? Explain.

a. You stand in front of a library from 4 P.M. to 6 P.M. to do a survey of who plans to vote for an upcoming tax for the library.

b. You stand in front of a library from open to close to do a survey of who plans to vote for an upcoming tax for the library.

21. A student's test scores in math are 95, 85, 75, 91, and 75. Compare the mean, median, and mode for the test scores. Which makes the grades look the highest? the lowest? Show your work and explain.

22. A class of 24 students was asked to identify a team sport in which they have participated. Their responses are shown in the line plot below. How many responses are recorded in the frequency table? How does this compare with the number of students polled? Explain how this could occur.

Number	Tally
Football	IIII
Soccer	THL III
Baseball	THL II
Basketball	THL
Tennis	IIII

Quarter 4 Test

Form D

Chapters 10–12

1. In which quadrant is the point with coordinates $(14, -13)$ located?

2. Write an ordered pair that is a solution of the equation $3x + 2y = -11$. Make sure that the x and y values in the ordered pair are integers less than 10 and greater than -10.

3. Without plotting points, explain which of these two equations is shown in the graph. $y = 2x - 1, y = -2x + 1$.

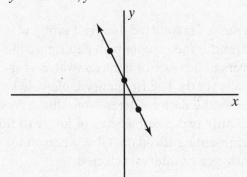

4. Write the absolute value equation shown by the graph below.

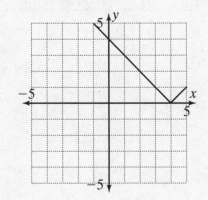

5. Point B below is translated up 4 units. What are its new coordinates?

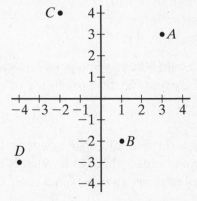

6. Draw a line of symmetry on this figure.

7. The figure on the left was rotated clockwise to the position shown on the right. How much was it rotated?

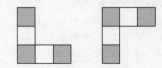

8. In the spreadsheet below, what balance belongs in cell C3?

	A	B	C
	Date	Deposit/Checks	Balance
1	6/25		$255
2	6/28	−$310	−$55
3	6/29	$165	

Chapters 10–12

9. Use a proportion to estimate the fish population.
Total fish counted: 1,151
Tagged fish counted: 99
Total tagged fish: 436

10. You toss a coin 30 times and get 12 heads. What is the experimental probability of getting heads?

11. A spinner is divided into eight congruent sections, numbered 1 through 8. What is the probability of spinning two 1s in a row?

12. How many ways can 4 books be placed on a shelf from a selection of 7 possible books?

13. Look at the stem-and-leaf plot below. How many students earned a score of 84?

Math Test Scores
```
9 | 2
8 | 4 4 5 6
7 | 2 2 5 5 8
6 | 0 1 2 5
```
Key: 6 | 2 means 62.

14. A cafe offers a choice of 5 different sandwiches, 4 different side dishes, and 6 different drinks for lunch. How many different lunches can be selected?

15. Which sample is more likely to be random? Explain.

   a. You walk through the halls of a school to do a survey.

   b. You stand at the entrance of the biology classroom to do a survey.

16. A student's test scores in history class are 92, 82, 75, 91, and 75. Compare the mean, median, and mode for the test scores. Which makes the grades look the highest? the lowest? Show your work and explain.

17. A survey conducted among a group of seventh-grade students to determine the average number of books a twelve-year-old reads yearly. The frequency table below shows the data collected from this survey. Identify two possible sizes of intervals for representing this data. Give a reason for each size of interval selected.

Number	1	2	3	4	5	6	7	8	9	10	11	12
Tally		||	||||		||	|||||		|||		||||||||		

Number	13	14	15	16	17	18	19	20	21	22	23	24
Tally		|||||||	||		|	||||	||	|||||||		||		||||

Quarter 4 Test

Chapters 10–12

Form E

1. In which quadrant is the point with coordinates $(-12, -11)$ located?

2. Determine if the ordered pair $(-4, 2)$ is a solution of $4x - 3y = -10$.

3. Without plotting points, explain which of these two equations is shown in the graph. $y = 6x - 1, y = -5x - 1$.

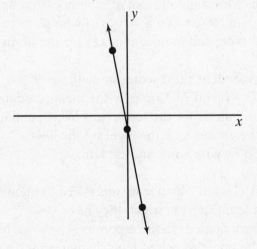

4. Graph $y = -x^2 + 4$ using integer values from -3 to 3.

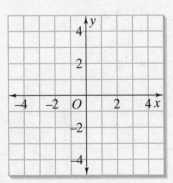

5. Point D below is translated down 2 units and to the right 5 units. What are its new coordinates?

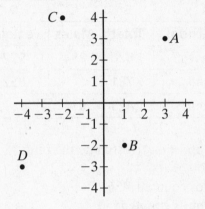

6. Draw a line of symmetry on the figure.

7. The figure on the left was rotated clockwise to the position shown on the right. How much was it rotated?

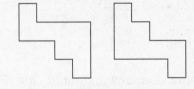

8. What number goes in cell C3 in the spreadsheet below?

	A	B	C	D
1	**High School**	**Total**	**Males**	**Females**
2	Southwest	1,826	854	972
3	Marshall	1,781		852
4	Washburn	1,423	631	

9. Use a proportion to estimate the bird population.
Total birds counted: 436
Banded birds counted: 50
Total banded birds: 70

10. A bag is filled with 4 tiles marked A, B, C, and D. What is the probability of *not* drawing a vowel out of the bag?

11. Seven red cubes and three green cubes are in a bag. Two cubes are chosen at random without replacement.
Find *P*(red, then green).

12. Calculate 6!.

13. Look at the stem-and-leaf plot below. How many students earned scores in the 70s or 80s?

Math Test Scores

```
9 | 2
8 | 4 4 5 6
7 | 2 2 5 5 8
6 | 0 1 2 5
```
Key: 7 | 5 means 75.

14. There are 5 students running for class president and 6 running for class vice president. How many different ways can a voter select one candidate for each office?

15. Which sample is more likely to be random? Explain.

a. You stand in front of a library from 4 P.M. to 6 P.M. to do a survey of who plans to vote for an upcoming tax for the library.

b. You stand in front of a library from open to close to do a survey of who plans to vote for an upcoming tax for the library.

16. A student's test scores in math are 95, 85, 75, 91, and 75. Compare the mean, median, and mode for the test scores. Which makes the grades look the highest? the lowest? Show your work and explain.

17. A class of 24 students was asked to identify a team sport in which they have participated. Their responses are shown in the line plot below. How many responses are recorded in the line plot? How does this compare with the number of students polled? Explain how this could occur.

Number	Tally
Football	IIII
Soccer	IHL III
Baseball	IHL II
Basketball	IHL
Tennis	IIII

Mid-Course Test .... **Form A**
Chapters 1–6

1. Estimate. $19.17 + $11.74

2. The original price for a swimsuit is $72.99. The sale price for the same swimsuit is $54.29. How much are you saving if you buy the swimsuit on sale?

3. A dessert cook purchased 14 cans of mixed fruit at $.85 each, 16 cans of light peaches at $.79 each, and 12 cans of light pears at $.79 each. What was the total cost of these purchases?

4. Change 4 kg 52 g to kilograms.

5. Write the integers 3, -13, 19, 17, -1, in order from least to greatest.

6. The elevation of the Salton Sea is -235 ft, while the elevation of Mount Shasta is 14,162 ft. Find the change in elevation from the Salton Sea to Mount Shasta.

7. A realty company showed an average profit-and-loss balance of $-$750$ per month for 3 months. Find the total balance for the 3 months.

8. You have a house lot that is 200 feet by 300 feet. You plan to build a house that is 70 ft $\times$ 100 ft. How much of the lot remains for the yard?

9. Simplify. $(6 + 2) \div 8 + 10$

10. What is the mode of the following set of data? 3, 6, 5, 8, 1, 5, 9, 5

11. Evaluate $9y - 4$ for $y = 6$.

12. Solve. $5x = 120$

13. A lab is using 155 mice to test a vaccine. Of these, 55 were injected with a 5-mg dose, and 42 with a 15-mg dose. The remaining mice make up the control group. Write an equation, and find the number of mice in the control group.

14. A number multiplied by a positive integer is -22. Explain what you know about the first number and why.

15. Write an algebraic expression for six more than three times a number.

Solve.

16. $2y + 9 = -3$

17. $\frac{x}{6} - 3 = 1$

18. A dietitian is preparing a dessert which contains 150 calories. This will be 60 calories less than $\frac{1}{2}$ the number of calories in a regular serving of apple pie and ice cream. How many calories are in a regular serving of apple pie and ice cream?

19. Write an inequality that represents "7 is greater than x."

Solve.

20. $t - 11 \leq 17$

21. $-30 > \frac{t}{-4}$

22. Simplify. $(7 - 2^2) + 3$

23. Write 5.93×10^3 in standard form.

24. What is the GCF of 60 and 84?

25. Write the fraction $\frac{18}{36}$ in simplest form.

26. Jennifer completed $\frac{13}{28}$ of a crossword puzzle. Liz completed $\frac{1}{2}$ of an identical puzzle. Who completed more of the puzzle?

27. What would be the perimeter of the fifth square in this pattern?

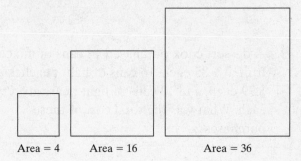

Area = 4　　　Area = 16　　　Area = 36

28. Write $6\frac{2}{3}$ as an improper fraction.

29. Order from least to greatest.
$\frac{1}{8}, 0.3, \frac{-2}{3}, -1$

30. You are baking muffins that require $\frac{1}{2}$ cup of vegetable oil. You only have $\frac{1}{3}$ cup left. How much more do you need?

31. A puppy weighs $4\frac{1}{8}$ pounds this week. Last week the puppy weighed $3\frac{3}{4}$ pounds. How much weight has the puppy gained this week?

Mid-Course Test (continued)

Chapters 1–6

32. You want to make $2\frac{1}{2}$ times the amount given by a recipe. The recipe calls for $1\frac{2}{3}$ cups of tomato sauce. How much tomato sauce should you use?

33. A carpenter has a box of nails, all the same size. One nail weights $\frac{1}{4}$ oz and all the nails weigh $64\frac{3}{4}$ oz. About how many nails are there?

34. Solve. $N + \frac{1}{2} = \frac{2}{3}$

35. Ben and Eric walked over to a neighbor's house to help with some yard work. Ben worked $\frac{2}{3}$ the amount of time that Eric worked. They started at 1:00 P.M., and Eric stopped at 4:45 P.M. At what time did Ben stop working?

36. $3\frac{3}{4}$ gallons = _____ pints

37. Choose the most appropriate metric unit of measure for the length of a paper clip.

38. There are 5 puppies and 9 kittens in a pet store. Write the ratio of puppies to kittens in 3 ways.

39. Use the data 4, 7, 12, 16, 17, 22, 25, and 28. Write the ratio of the sum of the even numbers to the sum of the odd numbers as a decimal. Round to the nearest tenth.

40. Which is the better buy, 3 cans for $2 or 6 cans for $5?

41. Write the *simplest* ratio that is equivalent to $\frac{16}{40}$.

42. A driver travels 190 miles in 4 hours. At that rate, how long will it take to drive 475 miles?

43. Two towns are 72 cm apart on a map with the scale 8 cm : 40 km. What is the actual distance between them?

44. What percent of the figure is shaded?

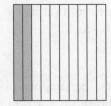

45. Order from least to greatest. $\frac{7}{12}$, 0.53, 72%, $\frac{2}{5}$

46. What percent of 45 is 18?

47. Enrollment at a middle school changed from 875 last year to 840 this year. What was the percent decrease?

48. Evaluate the expression $2^4 \cdot 3^2$.

49. Find the GCF of this pair of numbers. 63 and 84

50. Estimate. $34\frac{1}{8} \div 7\frac{2}{3}$

51. $\triangle TUV \sim \triangle WXY$. Find the length of side WY.

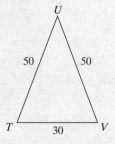
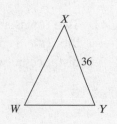

52. Give an example of a data set that has a mean of 48 and includes −8.

53. The diameter of Mercury, the smallest planet of the solar system, is about 3.1×10^3 miles. The largest planet's diameter, that of Jupiter, is about 8.8×10^4 miles. What is the difference between the diameters of these planets expressed in scientific notation?

54. Is 72,640 divisible by 8? Explain.

55. A salesperson earns a salary of $2,600 per month plus a 4% commission on all sales. How much will the salesperson earn if sales are $9,420 for the month? Show your work.

56. A holiday gift store is offering a seasonal set of cookie cutters for $6.50, plus 6% tax. There is also a $3.00 non-taxed shipping and handling charge. If you ordered a set of cookie cutters to be shipped to your home, what percent of the total payment would be for the cookie cutters only? Round to the nearest percent.

57. A plumber spends a total of 375 minutes on a job. The plumber is paid $42.50 per hour.

  a. Use mixed numbers to write the time spent in hours. Show your work.

  b. Estimate the amount the plumber is paid. Explain how you found your estimate.

58. A store manager has a salary of $57,480 and gets a raise of 3%. If the manager's expenses have increased by $1,700 is this raise enough to cover the expenses? If so, how much extra is there or how much extra has to be paid? Show your work.

Mid-Course Test

Chapters 1–6

1. Estimate using front-end estimation.

   57.36
   $\underline{+44.84}$

2. The original price for a mountain bike is $172.99. The sale price for the same mountain bike is $124.29. What are you saving if you buy the mountain bike on sale?

3. Water makes up about 0.6 of the weight of the human body. How much water is contained in a person who weighs 127.5 lb?

4. Change 3 kg 260 g to grams.

5. Write the integers 4, −12, 20, 16, and −2 in order from least to greatest.

6. A football team gained 2 yards on one play and lost 9 yards on the next play. Find the sum of the yardage for both plays.

7. A diver descended from the surface at a rate of −3 feet per second and reached the −60-foot level. Find how long it took the diver to reach this level.

8. You are making a board game for a class project. The gameboard will be 15 inches by 15 inches. A large square takes up 8 inches by 8 inches. How much of the gameboard area remains for decorations?

9. Simplify. $(10 - 3) \times 2 + 2$

10. What is the outlier of the following set of data? 2, 1, 0, 14, 3, 2, 0, 0

11. Evaluate $\frac{x}{y + z}$ for $x = 24$, $y = 4$, and $z = 2$.

12. Solve. $\frac{y}{8} = 24$

13. A concrete and gravel mixture will be used to fill a form with a volume of 1,500 m³. Write an equation, and find the volume of the gravel that must be mixed with 975 m³ of cement to fill the form.

14. Stuart solved the equation $\frac{x}{5} = -100$ and got $x = -20$. Explain how he might have gotten this answer. How would you help him correct his mistake?

15. Write an algebraic expression for 10 less than a number divided by 4.

Chapters 1–6

Solve.

16. $3y - 4 = 8$

17. $\frac{x}{5} + 6 = 10$

18. A nutritionist is preparing a casserole which contains 225 calories. This will be 20 calories less than $\frac{1}{4}$ the number of calories in a regular serving of casserole. How many calories are in a regular serving?

19. Write an inequality for "7 is less than or equal to *y*."

Solve.

20. $n + 5 \geq 7$

21. $-8y \geq -56$

22. Simplify. $3(4^2 - 5)$

23. Write 8.27×10^4 in standard form.

24. What is the GCF of 30 and 105?

25. Write the fraction $\frac{36}{90}$ in simplest form.

26. What is the area of the sixth rectangle in this pattern?

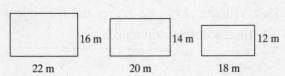

22 m   20 m   18 m

27. Write $3\frac{4}{7}$ as an improper fraction.

28. Order from least to greatest.
$\frac{-3}{4}, 0.6, \frac{2}{3}, -2$

29. A piece of fabric is $3\frac{1}{2}$ yards long. A pillow uses $1\frac{7}{8}$ yards. How much fabric will be left?

30. A bread recipe calls for $2\frac{1}{2}$ cups of white flour and $3\frac{2}{3}$ cups of whole wheat flour. How much flour is that all together?

31. A recipe calls for $\frac{2}{3}$ cup of chopped onion. How much onion is needed to make $\frac{3}{4}$ of the recipe amount?

32. Cement blocks $\frac{3}{4}$ ft long are being placed along one side of a walk that is $12\frac{3}{4}$ ft long. How many blocks are needed?

33. Solve and check. $x - \frac{2}{10} = \frac{3}{11}$

34. Ben and Eric walked over to a neighbor's house to help with some yard work. Ben worked $\frac{2}{3}$ the amount of time that Eric worked. They started at 12:30 P.M., and Eric stopped at 2:45 P.M. At what time did Ben stop working?

Mid-Course Test (continued)   Form B

Chapters 1–6

35. 19 ounces = _____ lb _____ oz

36. Choose the appropriate customary unit of measure for the capacity of a coffee mug.

37. There are 9 boys and 11 girls in the class. Write the ratio of boys to total students.

38. Use the data 4, 7, 12, 16, 17, 22, 25, and 28. Write the ratio of the sum of the odd numbers to the sum of the even numbers as a decimal. Round to the nearest tenth.

39. A farmer sells pumpkins for $4.00 each and the price drops to $2.50 for every pumpkin you buy after the third one. What is the average price per pumpkin if you buy ten?

40. Which is the best buy, 50 for $3.25 or 5 for $.38?

41. Write the simplest ratio that is equivalent to $\frac{27}{90}$.

42. Debbie saved $108 in 6 months. At that rate, how long will it take her to save the $360 she needs to buy a leather coat?

43. A scale model of an airplane uses the scale 1 in. = 8 ft. The model has a wingspan of 16.5 in. How wide is the actual wingspan?

44. What percent of the figure is shaded?

45. Order from least to greatest.

$0.89, 81\%, \frac{6}{7}, \frac{11}{13}$

46. What percent of 72 is 20?

47. A family is selling its condominium. The real estate agent's commission is 7%. The sellers want to have $69,750 left after the commission is deducted. What should the selling price be?

48. Evaluate the expression $12 + 7^2$.

49. Find the GCF of this pair of numbers. 24 and 40

50. Estimate. $3\frac{1}{8} \div \frac{2}{3}$

51. If the figures below are similar, what is the perimeter of the smaller figure?

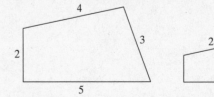

52. Give an example of a data set that has a median of 15 and includes −2.

53. The Pacific Ocean covers approximately 64,186,300 square miles of Earth's surface while the Atlantic Ocean stretches for about 33,420,000 square miles. Express both of these areas in scientific notation.

54. Is 8,592 divisible by 3? Explain.

55. A commissioned salesperson earns a weekly salary of $175 plus a 12% commission on all sales. How much will the salesperson earn for the week if sales for the week are $8,295? Show your work.

56. If you attend the dinner buffet between 4:00 P.M. and 6:00 P.M., the regular price of the buffet is reduced by 30%. Your family of four attends the buffet at 4:45 P.M. The regular price of the buffet is $10.50. How much does your family pay?

57. An electrician spends a total of 435 minutes on a job. The electrician is paid $45 per hour.

  a. Use mixed numbers to write the time spent in hours. Show your work.

  b. Estimate the amount the electrician is paid. Explain how you found your estimate.

58. A driver has a vehicle allowance of $7,800 per year. She received a 6% increase for the following year. If expenses for last year were $480 over her allowed amount, will she have enough this year based on her raise and the same expenses? If so, how much extra does she have to pay or how much extra will she save. Show your work.

Mid-Course Test
Chapters 1–6

Form D

1. Estimate. $19.17 + $11.74

2. The original price for a swimsuit is $72.99. The sale price for the same swimsuit is $54.29. How much are you saving if you buy the swimsuit on sale?

3. A dessert cook purchased 14 cans of mixed fruit at $.85 each, 16 cans of light peaches at $.79 each, and 12 cans of light pears at $.79 each. What was the total cost of these purchases?

4. Change 4 kg 52 g to kilograms.

5. Write the integers $3, -13, 19, 17, -1,$ in order from least to greatest.

6. The elevation of the Salton Sea is -235 ft, while the elevation of Mount Shasta is 14,162 ft. Find the change in elevation from the Salton Sea to Mount Shasta.

7. You have a house lot that is 200 feet by 300 feet. You plan to build a house that is 70 ft $\times$ 100 ft. How much of the lot remains for the yard?

8. Simplify. $(6 + 2) \div 8 + 10$

9. What is the mode of the following set of data? $3, 6, 5, 8, 1, 5, 9, 5$

10. Evaluate $9y - 4$ for $y = 6$.

11. Solve. $5x = 120$

12. A number multiplied by a positive integer is -22. Explain what you know about the first number and why.

13. Write an algebraic expression for six more than three times a number.

Solve.

14. $2y + 9 = -3$

15. $\frac{x}{6} - 3 = 1$

16. Write an inequality that represents "7 is greater than x."

Solve.

17. $t - 11 \leq 17$

18. $-30 > \frac{t}{-4}$

19. Simplify. $(7 - 2^2) + 3$

20. Write 5.93×10^3 in standard form.

21. What is the GCF of 60 and 84?

22. Write the fraction $\frac{18}{36}$ in simplest form.

23. What would be the perimeter of the fifth square in this pattern?

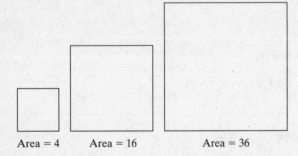

Area = 4   Area = 16   Area = 36

24. Write $6\frac{2}{3}$ as an improper fraction.

25. Order from least to greatest.
$\frac{1}{8}, 0.3, \frac{-2}{3}, -1$

26. Estimate. $2\frac{9}{11} + 4\frac{3}{7}$

27. You are baking muffins that require $\frac{1}{2}$ cup of vegetable oil. You only have $\frac{1}{3}$ cup left. How much more do you need?

28. A puppy weighs $4\frac{1}{8}$ pounds this week. Last week the puppy weighed $3\frac{3}{4}$ pounds. How much weight has the puppy gained this week?

29. You want to make $2\frac{1}{2}$ times the amount given by a recipe. The recipe calls for $1\frac{2}{3}$ cups of tomato sauce. How much tomato sauce should you use?

30. A carpenter has a box of nails, all the same size. One nail weights $\frac{1}{4}$ oz and all the nails weigh $64\frac{3}{4}$ oz. About how many nails are there?

Mid-Course Test (continued)

Form D

Chapters 1–6

31. Solve. $N + \frac{1}{2} = \frac{2}{3}$

32. Ben and Eric walked over to a neighbor's house to help with some yard work. Ben worked $\frac{2}{3}$ the amount of time that Eric worked. They started at 1:00 P.M., and Eric stopped at 4:45 P.M. At what time did Ben stop working?

33. $3\frac{3}{4}$ gallons = _____ pints

34. Choose the most appropriate metric unit of measure for the length of a paper clip.

35. There are 5 puppies and 9 kittens in a pet store. Write the ratio of puppies to kittens in 3 ways.

36. Which is the better buy, 3 cans for $2 or 6 cans for $5?

37. Write the *simplest* ratio that is equivalent to $\frac{16}{40}$.

38. A driver travels 190 miles in 4 hours. At that rate, how long will it take to drive 475 miles?

39. Two towns are 72 cm apart on a map with the scale 8 cm : 40 km. What is the actual distance between them?

40. What percent of the figure is shaded?

41. Order from least to greatest.
$\frac{7}{12}, 0.53, 72\%, \frac{2}{5}$

42. What percent of 45 is 18?

43. Enrollment at a middle school changed from 875 last year to 840 this year. What was the percent decrease?

44. Evaluate the expression $2^4 \cdot 3^2$.

45. Find the GCF of this pair of numbers. 63 and 84

46. Estimate. $34\frac{1}{8} \div 7\frac{2}{3}$

47. $\triangle TUV \sim \triangle WXY$. Find the length of side WY.

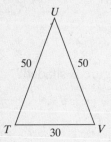
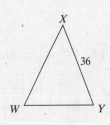

48. Find the mean of the data set:
$-8, -6, 14, 7, 1$.

49. Is 72,640 divisible by 8? Explain.

50. A salesperson earns a salary of $2,600 per month plus a 4% commission on all sales. How much will the salesperson earn if sales are $9,420 for the month? Show your work.

51. A plumber spends a total of 375 minutes on a job. The plumber is paid $42.50 per hour.

   a. Use mixed numbers to write the time spent in hours. Show your work.

   b. Estimate the amount the plumber is paid. Explain how you found your estimate.

52. A store manager has a salary of $57,480 and gets a raise of 3%. If the manager's expenses have increased by $1,700 is this raise enough to cover the expenses? If so, how much extra is there or how much extra has to be paid? Show your work.

Mid-Course Test

Chapters 1–6

Form E

1. Estimate using front-end estimation.
   57.36
   +44.84

2. The original price for a mountain bike is $172.99. The sale price for the same mountain bike is $124.29. What are you saving if you buy the mountain bike on sale?

3. Water makes up about 0.6 of the weight of the human body. How much water is contained in a person who weighs 127.5 lb?

4. Change 3 kg 260 g to grams.

5. Write the integers 4, -12, 20, 16, and -2 in order from least to greatest.

6. A football team gained 2 yards on one play and lost 9 yards on the next play. Find the sum of the yardage for both plays.

7. You are making a board game for a class project. The gameboard will be 15 inches by 15 inches. A large square takes up 8 inches by 8 inches. How much of the gameboard area remains for decorations?

8. Simplify. $(10 - 3) \times 2 + 2$

9. What is the outlier of the following set of data? 2, 1, 0, 14, 3, 2, 0, 0

10. Evaluate $\frac{x}{y + z}$ for $x = 24$, $y = 4$, and $z = 2$.

11. Solve. $\frac{y}{8} = 24$

12. Stuart solved the equation $\frac{x}{5} = -100$ and got $x = -20$. Explain how he might have gotten this answer. How would you help him correct his mistake?

13. Write an algebraic expression for 10 less than a number divided by 4.

Solve.

14. $3y - 4 = 8$

15. $\frac{x}{5} + 6 = 10$

16. Write an inequality for "7 is less than or equal to y."

Chapters 1–6

Solve.

17. $n + 5 \geq 7$

18. $-8y \geq -56$

19. Simplify. $3(4^2 - 5)$

20. Write 8.27×10^4 in standard form.

21. What is the GCF of 30 and 105?

22. Write the fraction $\frac{36}{90}$ in simplest form.

23. What is the area of the sixth rectangle in this pattern?

```
┌──────────┐
│          │ 16 m    ┌────────┐
│          │         │        │ 14 m   ┌──────┐
└──────────┘         │        │        │      │ 12 m
    22 m             └────────┘        └──────┘
                        20 m             18 m
```

24. Write $3\frac{4}{7}$ as an improper fraction.

25. Order from least to greatest.
    $\frac{-3}{4}, 0.6, \frac{2}{3}, -2$

26. Estimate. $5\frac{4}{5} + 2\frac{1}{7}$

27. A piece of fabric is $3\frac{1}{2}$ yards long. A pillow uses $1\frac{7}{8}$ yards. How much fabric will be left?

28. A bread recipe calls for $2\frac{1}{2}$ cups of white flour and $3\frac{2}{3}$ cups of whole wheat flour. How much flour is that all together?

29. A recipe calls for $\frac{2}{3}$ cup of chopped onion. How much onion is needed to make $\frac{3}{4}$ of the recipe amount?

30. Cement blocks $\frac{3}{4}$ ft long are being placed along one side of a walk that is $12\frac{3}{4}$ ft long. How many blocks are needed?

31. Solve and check. $x - \frac{2}{10} = \frac{3}{11}$

32. Ben and Eric walked over to a neighbor's house to help with some yard work. Ben worked $\frac{2}{3}$ the amount of time that Eric worked. They started at 12:30 P.M., and Eric stopped at 2:45 P.M. At what time did Ben stop working?

33. 19 ounces = _____ lb _____ oz

34. Choose the appropriate customary unit of measure for the capacity of a coffee mug.

Mid-Course Test (continued)

Chapters 1–6

Form E

35. There are 9 boys and 11 girls in the class. Write the ratio of boys to total students.

36. Which is the best buy, 50 for $3.25 or 5 for $.38?

37. Write the simplest ratio that is equivalent to $\frac{27}{90}$.

38. Debbie saved $108 in 6 months. At that rate, how long will it take her to save the $360 she needs to buy a leather coat?

39. A scale model of an airplane uses the scale 1 in. = 8 ft. The model has a wingspan of 16.5 in. How wide is the actual wingspan?

40. What percent of the figure is shaded?

41. Order from least to greatest.
$0.89, 81\%, \frac{6}{7}, \frac{11}{13}$

42. What percent of 72 is 20?

43. Evaluate the expression $12 + 7^2$.

44. Find the GCF of this pair of numbers. 24 and 40

45. Estimate. $3\frac{1}{8} \div \frac{2}{3}$

46. If the figures below are similar, what is the perimeter of the smaller figure?

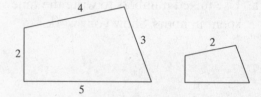

47. Find the median of the data set: $-2, 10, 15, 23, 32$.

48. The Pacific Ocean covers approximately 64,186,300 square miles of Earth's surface while the Atlantic Ocean stretches for about 33,420,000 square miles. Express both of these areas in scientific notation.

49. Is 8,592 divisible by 3? Explain.

50. A commissioned salesperson earns a weekly salary of $175 plus a 12% commission on all sales. How much will the salesperson earn for the week if sales for the week are $8,295? Show your work.

51. An electrician spends a total of 435 minutes on a job. The electrician is paid $45 per hour.

  a. Use mixed numbers to write the time spent in hours. Show your work.

  b. Estimate the amount the electrician is paid. Explain how you found your estimate.

52. A driver has a vehicle allowance of $7,800 per year. She received a 6% increase for the following year. If expenses for last year were $480 over her allowed amount, will she have enough this year based on her raise and the same expenses? If so, how much extra does she have to pay or how much extra will she save. Show your work.

Final Test

Form A

Chapters 1–12

1. Round to estimate.
   $3.79 + 2.99 + 1.07$

2. A hobbyist bought $18.07 of craft materials. She gave the sales clerk $20.27. How much money did the hobbyist receive as change?

3. A chef sold pizzas that cost $7.98 to make. If she sold 18 pizzas at a fair, how much money did she spend on the cost of the materials?

4. A football team gained 4 yards on one play and lost 9 yards on the next play. Find the team's total yardage on the two plays.

5. Order the following integers from greatest to least. $-12, 20, -11, 0$

6. A neighbor wants to buy a new stereo that costs $340. He will be able to save $17 per week in order to buy it. Write and solve an equation to find the number of weeks before he can get the new stereo.

7. Solve. $9 = \frac{r}{2} - 3$

8. Write a sentence for the equation $3p = -27$.

9. Graph $3 < x + 7$ on the number line.

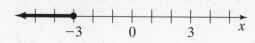

10. Write an inequality for the graph below.

11. Write the *simplest* fraction equivalent to $\frac{24}{27}$.

12. Simplify. $3^2 + 4(8 - 5)$

13. Show that $\frac{2}{3} < \frac{3}{4}$ is a true statement by changing the fractions to decimals.

14. Write the prime factorization of 126. Use exponents where possible.

15. A runner ran $3\frac{3}{4}$ miles the first day of the race, $6\frac{1}{2}$ miles the second day of the race, and $5\frac{1}{5}$ miles the third day of the race. How many total miles did he run?

16. Granola bars that weigh $2\frac{1}{3}$ oz each are packed 12 to a box. How much do all the granola bars in a box weigh?

17. An art teacher has a $12\frac{3}{4}$-oz jar of tempera paint. He wants to divide it equally among 6 students. How much should he give to each student?

18. Solve for x. $x + \frac{3}{4} = \frac{5}{6}$

19. $84 \text{ oz} = $ _____ lb _____ oz

20. A drama class consists of 11 boys and 16 girls. Write the ratio of girls to boys in three ways.

21. The state of Georgia is made up of 159 counties and 58,056 square miles. What is the unit rate of square miles per county? Round your answer to the nearest mile.

22. Which is the better buy?
$23.23 for 9 cans of chili
$19.60 for 8 cans of chili

23. Does the pair of ratios below form a proportion? Explain by finding a common denominator.
$\frac{11}{19} \stackrel{?}{=} \frac{55}{95}$

24. $\triangle XYZ \sim \triangle JKL$. Find the length of the missing side.

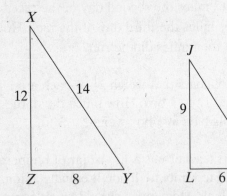

25. Write the following in order from least to greatest.
$72\%, \frac{7}{9}, 0.79, \frac{11}{15}$

26. Write 0.9% as a decimal and a fraction.

27. 33 is what percent of 50? If necessary, round the answer to the nearest tenth.

28. 25% of what number is 67?

29. What is the total cost of a coat priced at $86.90 if there is a 7% sales tax?

30. Find the area of this figure.

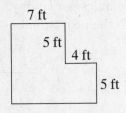

31. a. Name a pair of complementary angles.
b. Which line is perpendicular to $\overleftrightarrow{EF}$?
c. Name a pair of parallel lines.

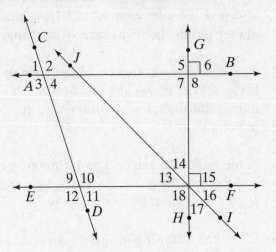

32. Use the circle below. Point X is the center of the circle. Classify $\triangle BXD$ by its angles and its sides.

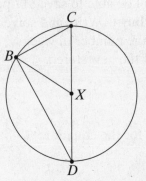

33. A triangle is congruent to the one shown below. What is the measure of its angle that is congruent to $\angle NLM$?

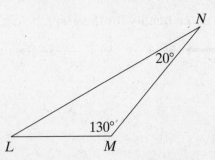

Final Test (continued)

Chapters 1–12

Form A

34. Eighty percent of the days in a town are clear, and the rest are cloudy. Tell what central angle you would draw on a circle graph to show how many clear days there were.

35. Find the area of the trapezoid.

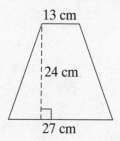

13 cm

24 cm

27 cm

36. Find the length of the missing side.

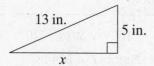

13 in.

5 in.

x

37. Find the volume of a cylinder that has a diameter of 14 feet and a height of 12 feet. Round to the nearest cubic foot.

38. Find the surface area of the triangular prism. Round to the nearest tenth.

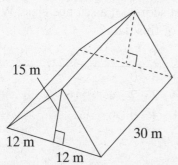

15 m

12 m

30 m

12 m

39. What is the approximate length of each edge of a cube with a volume of 150 cm^3? Round to the nearest tenth of a centimeter.

40. How are cones and pyramids alike? How are they different?

41. Complete the function table.

input (n)	output ($n - 5$)
2	
3	
4	

42. Describe an activity that could be represented by this graph.

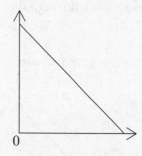

0

43. The graph below illustrates the average speeds of whales and barracuda. Write a rule to represent distance as a function of time for each animal.

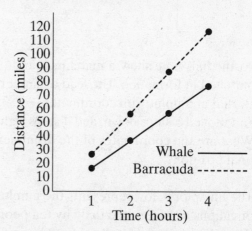

Whale ———
Barracuda - - - - - -

Distance (miles)

Time (hours)

44. On your sixth birthday, your family deposits $100 in an account that pays 5% interest, compounded annually. How much is in the account on the day you turn 13?

45. In which quadrant are both coordinates of a point negative?

46. Used paperback books are on sale for $.75 each. How many books could you buy if you had $3.75? Complete the table to find your answer.

x				
y				

47. Find the slope of a road if a line graph representing the road passes through the points $(5, 3)$ and $(25, 8)$.

48. Write an equation for the graph shown below.

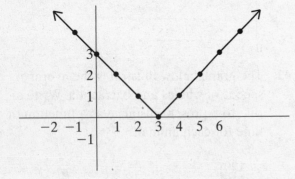

49. At the half-time show, a marching band marched in formation. The lead drummer started at a point with coordinates $(-1, 3)$ and moved 5 steps down, and 4 steps right. What are the coordinates of the drummer's final position?

50. The line plot below represents the number of gallons of water used daily by ten people. Write the number of gallons used by each of the ten people.

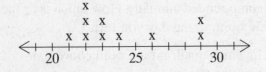

51. The double-bar graph below compares the number of fiction and non-fiction books in three different elementary school libraries. What is the difference between the number of fiction and non-fiction books in School C's library according to the graph?

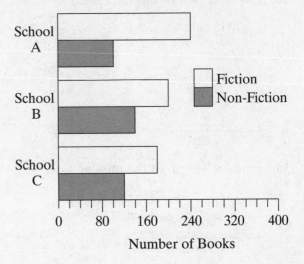

52. What type of graph is best suited for display of the populations of boys and girls at three different schools?

53. The stem-and-leaf plot below was created to show the test scores of a science class. What is the mean of this data?

Stem	Leaf
10	0 0 0 0
9	0 0 2 2 4 6 6 8 8
8	0 4 4 6 6

Key: $9 \mid 2 = 92$

54. After the introduction of a new fruit drink, a taste test is conducted to see how it is being received. Of those who participated, 64 said they preferred the new fruit drink, 112 preferred the old fruit drink, and 24 could not tell any difference. What is the probability that a person in this survey preferred the new fruit drink?

Final Test

Form B

Chapters 1–12

1. Round to estimate.
   $4.26 + 5.37 + 2.79$

2. Paul had $67.55. He spent $28.77. How much money did he have left?

3. A friend sold bird houses that cost $6.29 to make. If she sold 15 bird houses at the craft show, how much did she spend on the cost of materials?

4. What is the change in elevation in going from an elevation of -175 m to 750 m?

5. Order the following integers from least to greatest. $-15, 30, -17, 5$

6. Your brother spent $800 on a vacation tour package and then spent an average of $30 each day he was on the tour. In all, he spent $1,040 for the entire vacation tour. Write and solve an equation to find how many days the tour was.

7. Solve for j. $5 = 6j + 41$

8. Write a sentence for the equation $x - 4 = -3$.

9. Graph $4 \geq x + 5$ on the number line.

10. Write an inequality for the graph below.

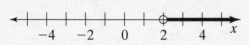

11. Write the *simplest* fraction equivalent to $\frac{24}{36}$.

12. Simplify. $(3 + 9)2 + 7 \times 3^2$

13. Show that $\frac{5}{6} < \frac{7}{8}$ by changing the numbers to fractions with least common denominators.

14. Write the prime factorization of 735. Use exponents when possible.

15. A pattern for drapes requires $4\frac{1}{2}$ yd of fabric. A pattern for a matching bedspread requires $3\frac{1}{4}$ yd of fabric. How much fabric is needed to make both of these items?

16. A classmate has collected 420 baseball cards. If his brother has collected $2\frac{1}{2}$ times as many cards as the classmate has, how many cards does the brother have?

17. How many $2\frac{1}{4}$-ft boards can be cut from a $13\frac{1}{2}$-ft board?

18. Your aunt bought $2\frac{2}{3}$ pounds of carrots at the store. She wants to divide the carrots among her friends, giving each friend $\frac{1}{3}$ pound. How many friends can she share with?

19. 88 ft = _____ yds _____ft

20. A bunch of flowers consists of 19 daisies and 14 carnations. Write the ratio of carnations to daisies in three ways.

21. Write a unit rate equivalent to $\frac{80 \text{ feet}}{20 \text{ seconds}}$.

22. Which is the better buy?
$1.79 for an 18-ounce bag of pretzels
$3.50 for a 36-ounce bag of pretzels

23. Does the pair of ratios below form a proportion? Explain by finding a common denominator.
$\frac{42}{56} \overset{?}{=} \frac{6}{7}$

24. The ratio of the corresponding sides of the similar figures is 3 : 2. What is the length of Side *A*?

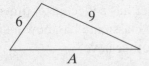 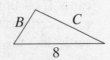

25. Write the following in order from least to greatest.
$\frac{11}{24}, 0.39, 42\%, \frac{2}{5}$

26. Write 120% as a decimal and a fraction.

27. 82 is what percent of 194? If necessary, round the answer to the nearest tenth.

28. 35% of what number is 280?

29. What is the total cost of a meal if the check is for $13.34 and you want to leave a 15% tip?

30. Find the area of this figure.

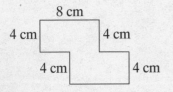

31. **a.** Name a pair of perpendicular lines.

b. Which lines are parallel?

c. Name a pair of supplementary angles.

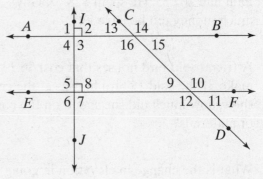

32. Use the circle below. Point *Y* is the center of the circle. $\overline{BC} = \overline{YB}$. Classify $\triangle BYC$ by its angles and its sides.

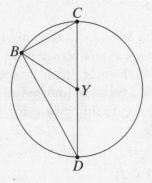

33. What is the perimeter of a triangle which is congruent to the one shown below?

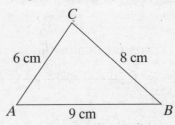

Final Test (continued)   Form B

Chapters 1–12

34. Forty percent of the plants bought by a gardener were roses. Twenty percent of the plants were pansies. The rest of the plants were grasses. Find the central angles of a circle graph which shows each of these percents.

35. Find the area of the parallelogram below.

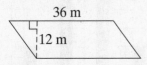

36. Find the length of the missing side.

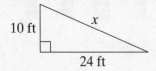

37. Find the volume of a cylinder that has a diameter of 22 feet and a height of 14 feet. Round to the nearest cubic foot.

38. Find the volume of the triangular prism.

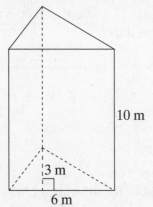

39. The volume of a cube is 1,331 in.^{3}. What is the area of each face? Round to the nearest square inch.

40. How are prisms and pyramids alike? How are they different?

41. Complete the function table.

input (n)	output ($n + 2$)
1	
3	
7	

42. Describe a real-world situation that could be represented by the graph below.

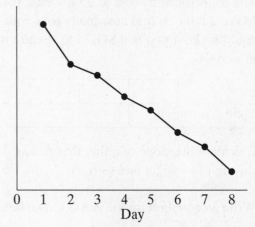

43. Refer to the graph below. How far would a barracuda travel in 6 hours? How long would it take a whale to travel this same distance?

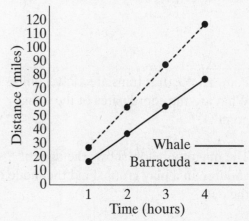

44. You borrow $200 from a relative for six months. You agree to pay compound interest as the rate of 1% per month. How much interest will you pay your relative when you return the money at the end of six months?

45. In which quadrant is the *x*-coordinate negative and the *y*-coordinate positive?

46. Materials for a toy cost $2.25 for each toy. Make a table to find how many toys you could make if you had $11.25 to spend on materials.

x					
y					

47. Calculate the slope of a line that passes through the origin and $(-6, 3)$.

48. Write an equation for the graph shown below.

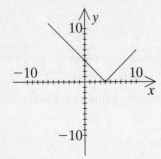

49. Point $A(-3, 0)$ is translated left 3 units. What are the coordinates of the image point A'?

50. The line plot below shows the ages of children in a play group. Find the mode of the data.

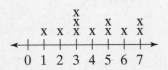

51. Which page has the most black ink on it?

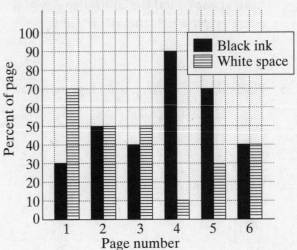

Amount of Black Ink and White Space on Pages of Print

52. What type of graph is best suited for display of the monthly sales of two different types of cars during a one-year period?

53. The stem-and-leaf plot below was created to show the test scores of a science class. What is the mode of this data?

Stem	Leaf
10	0 0 0 0
9	0 0 2 2 4 6 6 8 8
8	0 4 4 6 6

Key: 9 | 2 = 92

54. Give the probability for drawing a blue marker from a bag containing 7 blue markers and 3 white markers. Express the probability as a fraction, a percent, and a decimal.

Final Test

Form D

Chapters 1–12

1. Round to estimate.
   $3.79 + 2.99 + 1.07$

2. A hobbyist bought $18.07 of craft materials. She gave the sales clerk $20.27. How much money did the hobbyist receive as change?

3. A chef sold pizzas that cost $7.98 to make. If she sold 18 pizzas at a fair, how much money did she spend on the cost of the materials?

4. A football team gained 4 yards on one play and lost 9 yards on the next play. Find the team's total yardage on the two plays.

5. Order the following integers from greatest to least. $-12, 20, -11, 0$

6. Solve. $9 = \frac{r}{2} - 3$

7. Graph $3 < x + 7$ on the number line.

   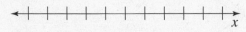

8. Write an inequality for the graph below.

   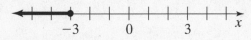

9. Write the *simplest* fraction equivalent to $\frac{24}{27}$.

10. Simplify. $3^2 + 4(8 - 5)$

11. Show that $\frac{2}{3} < \frac{3}{4}$ is a true statement by changing the fractions to decimals.

12. Write the prime factorization of 126. Use exponents where possible.

13. A runner ran $3\frac{3}{4}$ miles the first day of the race, $6\frac{1}{2}$ miles the second day of the race, and $5\frac{1}{5}$ miles the third day of the race. How many total miles did he run?

14. Granola bars that weigh $2\frac{1}{3}$ oz each are packed 12 to a box. How much do all the granola bars in a box weigh?

15. An art teacher has a $12\frac{3}{4}$-oz jar of tempera paint. He wants to divide it equally among 6 students. How much should he give to each student?

16. Solve for x. $x + \frac{3}{4} = \frac{5}{6}$

17. $84 \text{ oz} = \underline{\hspace{1cm}} \text{ lb} \underline{\hspace{1cm}} \text{oz}$

18. A drama class consists of 11 boys and 16 girls. Write the ratio of girls to boys in three ways.

19. Which is the better buy?
$23.23 for 9 cans of chili
$19.60 for 8 cans of chili

20. Does the pair of ratios below form a proportion? Explain by finding a common denominator.

$$\frac{11}{19} \stackrel{?}{=} \frac{55}{95}$$

21. $\triangle XYZ \sim \triangle JKL$. Find the length of the missing side.

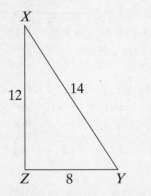

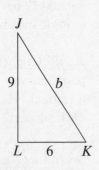

22. Write the following in order from least to greatest.

$72\%, \frac{7}{9}, 0.79, \frac{11}{15}$

23. Write 0.9% as a decimal and a fraction.

24. 33 is what percent of 50? If necessary, round the answer to the nearest tenth.

25. 25% of what number is 67?

26. What is the total cost of a coat priced at $86.90 if there is a 7% sales tax?

27. a. Name a pair of complementary angles.

b. Which line is perpendicular to $\overleftrightarrow{EF}$?

c. Name a pair of parallel lines.

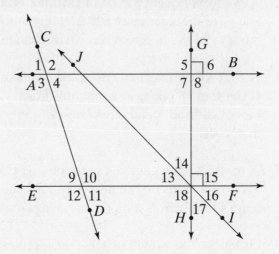

28. Use the circle below. Point X is the center of the circle. Classify $\triangle BXD$ by its angles and its sides.

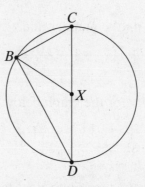

29. A triangle is congruent to the one shown below. What is the measure of its angle that is congruent to $\angle NLM$?

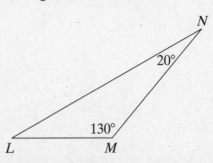

Final Test (continued)

Form D

Chapters 1–12

30. Eighty percent of the days in a town are clear, and the rest are cloudy. Tell what central angle you would draw on a circle graph to show how many clear days there were.

31. Find the area of the trapezoid.

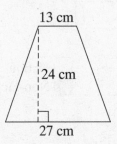

13 cm

24 cm

27 cm

32. Find the length of the missing side.

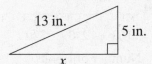

13 in.

5 in.

x

33. Find the volume of a cylinder that has a diameter of 14 feet and a height of 12 feet. Round to the nearest cubic foot.

34. Find the surface area of the triangular prism.

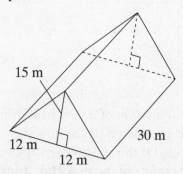

15 m

12 m

12 m

30 m

35. How are cones and pyramids alike? How are they different?

36. Complete the function table.

input (n)	output ($n - 5$)
2	
3	
4	

37. The graph below illustrates the average speeds of whales and barracuda. Write a rule to represent distance as a function of time for each animal.

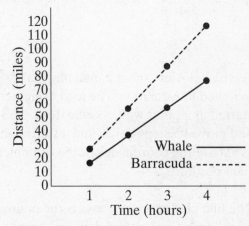

Whale ———
Barracuda --------

38. On your sixth birthday, your family deposits $100 in an account that pays 5% interest, compounded annually. How much is in the account on the day you turn 13?

39. In which quadrant are both coordinates of a point negative?

40. Find the slope of a road if a line graph representing the road passes through the points $(5, 3)$ and $(25, 8)$.

41. Write an equation for the graph shown below.

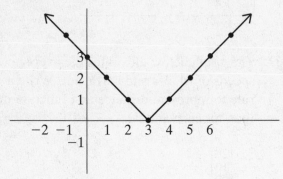

42. At the half-time show, a marching band marched in formation. The lead drummer started at a point with coordinates $(-1, 3)$ and moved 5 steps down, and 4 steps right. What are the coordinates of the drummer's final position?

43. The line plot below represents the number of gallons of water used daily by ten people. Write the number of gallons used by each of the ten people.

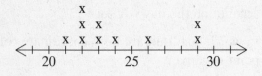

44. The double-bar graph below compares the number of fiction and non-fiction books in three different elementary school libraries. What is the difference between the number of fiction and non-fiction books in School C's library according to the graph?

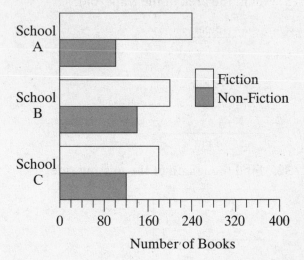

45. The stem-and-leaf plot below was created to show the test scores of a science class. What is the mean of this data?

Stem	Leaf
10	0 0 0 0
9	0 0 2 2 4 6 6 8 8
8	0 4 4 6 6

Key: $9 \mid 2 = 92$

46. After the introduction of a new fruit drink, a taste test is conducted to see how it is being received. Of those who participated, 64 said they preferred the new fruit drink, 112 preferred the old fruit drink, and 24 could not tell any difference. What is the probability that a person in this survey preferred the new fruit drink?

Final Test

Chapters 1–12

Form E

1. Round to estimate.
   4.26 + 5.37 + 2.79

2. Paul had $67.55. He spent $28.77. How much money did he have left?

3. A friend sold bird houses that cost $6.29 to make. If she sold 15 bird houses at the craft show, how much did she spend on the cost of materials?

4. What is the change in elevation in going from an elevation of -175 m to 750 m?

5. Order the following integers from least to greatest. $-15, 30, -17, 5$

6. Solve for j. $5 = 6j + 41$

7. Graph $4 \geq x + 5$ on the number line.

8. Write an inequality for the graph below.

9. Write the *simplest* fraction equivalent to $\frac{24}{36}$.

10. Simplify. $(3 + 9)2 + 7 \times 3^2$

11. Show that $\frac{5}{6} < \frac{7}{8}$ by changing the numbers to fractions with least common denominators.

12. Write the prime factorization of 220. Use exponents when possible.

13. A pattern for drapes requires $4\frac{1}{2}$ yd of fabric. A pattern for a matching bedspread requires $3\frac{1}{4}$ yd of fabric. How much fabric is needed to make both of these items?

14. A classmate has collected 420 baseball cards. If his brother has collected $2\frac{1}{2}$ times as many cards as the classmate has, how many cards does the brother have?

15. How many $2\frac{1}{4}$-ft boards can be cut from a $13\frac{1}{2}$-ft board?

16. Your aunt bought $2\frac{2}{3}$ pounds of carrots at the store. She wants to divide the carrots among her friends, giving each friend $\frac{1}{3}$ pound. How many friends can she share with?

17. 88 ft = _____ yds _____ ft

18. A bunch of flowers consists of 19 daisies and 14 carnations. Write the ratio of carnations to daisies in three ways.

19. Which is the better buy?
$1.79 for an 18-ounce bag of pretzels
$3.50 for a 36-ounce bag of pretzels

20. Does the pair of ratios below form a proportion? Explain by finding a common denominator.

$$\frac{42}{56} \stackrel{?}{=} \frac{6}{7}$$

21. The ratio of the corresponding sides of the similar figures is 3 : 2. What is the length of Side A?

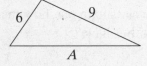

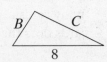

22. Write the following in order from least to greatest.

$\frac{11}{24}, 0.39, 42\%, \frac{2}{5}$

23. Write 120% as a decimal and a fraction.

24. 82 is what percent of 205?

25. 35% of what number is 280?

26. What is the total cost of a meal if the check is for $13.34 and you want to leave a 15% tip?

27. a. Name a pair of perpendicular lines.

b. Which lines are parallel?

c. Name a pair of supplementary angles.

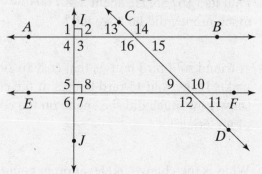

28. Use the circle below. Point Y is the center of the circle. $BC = YB$. Classify $\triangle BYC$ by its angles and its sides.

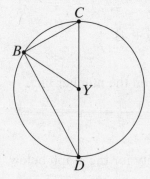

29. What is the perimeter of a triangle which is congruent to the one shown below?

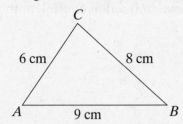

Final Test (continued)

Chapters 1–12

30. Forty percent of the plants bought by a gardener were roses. Twenty percent of the plants were pansies. The rest of the plants were grasses. Find the central angles of a circle graph which shows each of these percents.

31. Find the area of the parallelogram below.

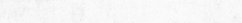
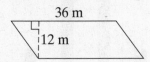

36 m

12 m

32. Find the length of the missing side.

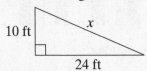

10 ft x

24 ft

33. Find the surface area of a cylinder that has a diameter of 22 feet and a height of 14 feet. Round to the nearest cubic foot.

34. Find the volume of the triangular prism.

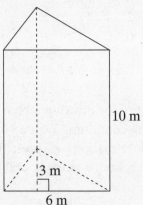

10 m

3 m

6 m

35. How are prisms and pyramids alike? How are they different?

36. Complete the function table.

input (n)	output ($n + 2$)
1	
3	
7	

37. Refer to the graph below. How far would a barracuda travel in 6 hours? How long would it take a whale to travel this same distance?

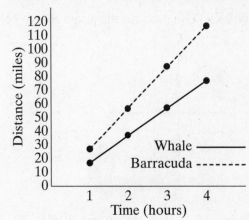

38. You borrow $200 from a relative for six months. You agree to pay compound interest as the rate of 1% per month. How much interest will you pay your relative when you return the money at the end of six months?

39. In which quadrant is the *x*-coordinate negative and the *y*-coordinate positive?

40. Calculate the slope of a line that passes through the origin and $(-6, 3)$.

41. Write an equation for the graph shown below.

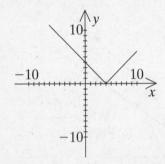

42. Point $A(-3, 0)$ is translated left 3 units. What are the coordinates of the image point A'?

43. The line plot below shows the ages of children in a play group. Find the mode of the data.

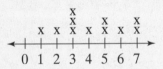

44. Which page has the most black ink on it?

Amount of Black Ink and White Space on Pages of Print

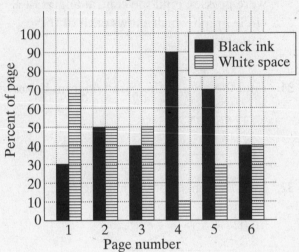

45. The stem-and-leaf plot below was created to show the test scores of a science class. What is the mode of this data?

Stem	Leaf
10	0 0 0 0
9	0 0 2 2 4 6 6 8 8
8	0 4 4 6 6

Key: 9 | 2 = 92

46. Give the probability for drawing a blue marker from a bag containing 7 blue markers and 3 white markers. Express the probability as a fraction, a percent, and a decimal.

Name _____ Class _____ Date _____

Writing Gridded Responses
....
Exercises

Write what you would grid for each answer. Then grid your answers on grids provided by your teacher.

1. Simplify 8(3.6). _____

2. Find the sum of 4.23 and 8.43. _____

3. Find the sum of 12.34 and 45.32. _____

4. Find the difference between 6.8 and −3.4. _____

5. Find $1\frac{1}{2} \div \frac{5}{8}$. _____

6. Solve the proportion. $\frac{4}{12} = \frac{n}{6}$ _____

7. Find the mean of the data set. 3 5 2 9 8 5 3 _____

8. Find the next number in the sequence: 3, −6, 12, −24, ... _____

9. To get to your grandfather's office, you have to walk up 8 flights of stairs each containing 10 steps. How many steps do you walk up?

_____

10. You have $340 in a bank account. You have decided to add $8 per week to your account for the next seven weeks. What is your balance at the end of four weeks?

_____

11. A carpenter cuts a 6-m board into 4 equal pieces. What is the length in centimeters of each piece?

_____

12. You spent $14.32 on scrapbook stickers. If each package of stickers cost $1.79, how many packages of stickers did you buy?

_____

13. For your birthday you receive $30. If you buy a CD for $12.99 and a magazine for $4.95, how much money do you have left?

_____

14. Software for Mr. Key's new computer costs the following: word processing $350, additional graphics $34.99, and tax software $79.99. What is the total cost of the software to the nearest dollar?

_____

15. Margaret can type at a rate of 30 words per minute. At this rate, how long would it take her to type 450 words?

_____

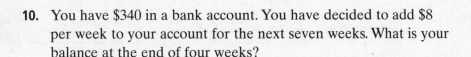

Writing Short Responses

Exercises

Use the scoring rubric below to answer each question.

Scoring Rubric

2 The equation and the solution are correct.

1 There is no equation, but there is a method to show how the answer was achieved.

1 There is an equation and a solution, both of which may contain minor errors. The solution indicates the answer, but does not show units.

0 There is no response, it is completely incorrect, or it is the correct response but there is no procedure shown.

---

1. During a summer special, costs for bowling at the Swanton Sports Center are $2.75 for shoe rental and $1.50 for each game bowled. Mindy spent $8.75. Write and solve an equation to find how many games she bowled.

2 points	1 point	0 points
Let x = number of games. $2.75 + 1.50x = 8.75$ $1.50x = 6.00$ $\dfrac{1.50x}{1.50} = \dfrac{6.00}{1.50}$ $x = 4$ Mindy played 4 games.	$2.75 + 1.50x = 8.75$ $1.50x = 6.00$ $x = 9$ 9 games	3 games

a. Explain why each response above received the indicated points.

_____

_____

_____

b. Write a 1-point response that does not have an equation.

_____

2. While school shopping Marcus spent a total of $63.93. His purchase included a new pair of jeans for $21.99 and some T-shirts for $6.99 each.

2 points	1 point	0 points
	$6.99t - 21.99 = 63.93$ $6.99t = 85.92$ $t = 12.29$ 12 T-shirts	7 T-shirts

a. Write and solve an equation to find how many T-shirts he bought.

b. Write a 2-point response.

Reading for Understanding

Exercises

Use the passage to complete exercises 1–4.

Cedar Point in Sandusky, Ohio, boasts one of the tallest roller coasters in the United States. The Millennium Force measures in at 310 feet. After riders reach the top of the first hill, they plunge 93 miles per hour down a 300-foot drop at an 80-degree angle. For the 2-minute, 20-second ride, riders are seated in one of three 36-passenger trains and travel along its 6,595-foot-long track.

1. How tall is the Millennium Force's tallest hill?

   _____

2. How many seconds does each ride take?

   _____

3. The three trains together can complete about 44 rides in an hour. How many passengers can ride in one hour?

   _____

4. How many miles long is the track? (Hint: 5,280 feet = 1 mile)

   _____

Use the passage to complete exercises 5–7.

The giraffe is one of the heaviest land animals. Large males can weigh up to 1,900 kg. Females are smaller and rarely reach half the weight of the males. A giraffe's neck and long legs combine to make the giraffe one of the tallest of all animals, averaging about 17 feet tall for a male. The giraffe's neck, supported by seven elongated vertebrae, can measure even longer than its 1.8-m (6-ft) legs. A giraffe's long legs give it the ability to run at a top speed of about 56 km/h (35 mi/h).

5. What is the weight of a large giraffe in pounds? (Hint: There are 2.2 pounds per kilogram.)

   _____

6. What is the weight of a female giraffe, in kilograms?

   _____

7. How far could a giraffe travel at its top speed in fifteen minutes?

   _____

Writing Extended Responses

Exercises

Use the scoring rubric shown to answer each question.

Scoring Rubric

4 Identifies the variables, shows all work, and answers all parts of the problem.

3 Identifies the variable, shows work, and answers all parts of the problem. There may be a computational error.

1 Problem set up incorrectly, does not answer all parts of the problem and contains errors.

1. Parts to fix your truck cost you $115.95. The mechanic charges $42 per hour for labor. The final bill you receive is $241.95. How long did the mechanic work on your truck? Write and solve an equation. Show all your work.

4 points	3 points
Let h = hours worked.	Let h = hours worked.
$42h + 115.95 = 241.95$	$42h + 115.95 = 241.95$
$42h + 115.95 - 115.95 = 241.95 - 115.95$	$42h = 357.90$
$42h = 126$	$\frac{42h}{42} = \frac{357.90}{42}$
$\frac{42h}{42} = \frac{126}{42}$	$h = 8.5$
$h = 3$	8.5 hours
The mechanic worked a total of 3 hours on the truck.	

   a. Read the 3-point response. What error was made?

   _____

   _____

   b. Write what you think a 2-point response to the problem would look like.

   _____

2. Aaron works at Hobby Town and has 256 purple bracelet beads and 96 orange bracelet beads to repackage. Each new bag must contain the same number of purple beads and the same number of orange beads. Aaron wants to make as many bags as possible. How many bags can he make? How many beads of each color will Aaron put in each new bag?

   a. Write a 4-point response to the problem.

   _____

   _____

   _____

   b. Write a 1-point response to the problem.

   _____

Using a Variable

Exercises

Use a variable to write an equation and solve each problem.

1. A lunch platter contains a variety of luncheon meats. To serve 12 people, $3\frac{1}{2}$ pounds of meat are needed. How many pounds of meat are needed to serve 18 people?

   _____

2. If 80 kg of cement are used to make 400 kg of concrete, how much cement is needed to make 1,600 kg of concrete?

   _____

3. A machine produces 2,070 flashlights in 8.5 hours. How many flashlights will the machine produce in 40 hours?

   _____

4. You receive $72.96 for working an 8-hour day. How much would you receive for working a 32-hour week?

   _____

5. A clothing manufacturer is shipping sweaters to a department store. The manufacturer has previously shipped 330 sweaters in 18 boxes. At this rate, how many boxes would the manufacturer need to ship 550 sweaters?

   _____

6. The monthly payment on a loan is $29.50 for every $1,000 borrowed. At this rate, find the monthly payment for a $9,000 car loan.

   _____

7. Nine ceramic tiles are required to cover four square feet. At this rate, how many square feet can be tiled with 270 ceramic tiles?

   _____

8. A quality control inspector found three defective computer chips in a shipment of 500 chips. At this rate, how many computer chips would be defective in a shipment of 3,000 chips?

   _____

9. The ratio of chicory to coffee in a New England coffee mixture is 1 : 8. If the coffee company uses 85 pounds of chicory for a batch of coffee mixture, how many pounds of coffee are needed?

   _____

10. In preparing a banquet for 30 people, a restaurant cook uses nine pounds of potatoes. How many pounds of potatoes will be needed for a banquet for 175 people?

    _____

© Pearson Education, Inc., publishing as Pearson Prentice Hall.

Working Backward

Exercises

Solve each problem by working backward. Circle the correct answer.

1. Your grades on five math tests are 95, 86, 79, 88, and 93. What grade do you need on the sixth test to have an average of 90?

    A. 76   **B.** 90   **C.** 99   **D.** 100

2. The surface area of a cube is 294 square feet. What is the length (in feet) of each edge of the cube? [Hint: $S = 6s^2$]

    F. -7 feet   **G.** 7 feet   **H.** 49 feet   **J.** 64 feet

3. If $7x - 17 = 32$, what is the value of x?

    A. 2.14   **B.** 5   **C.** 7   **D.** 9

4. What is the greatest number of theater tickets you can buy if you have $227.18 and each theater ticket costs $42.75?

    F. 4 tickets   **G.** 5 tickets   **H.** 6 tickets   **J.** 7 tickets

5. If you start with a number, multiply by 3, then subtract 16, the result is 152. What is the number?

    A. 37   **B.** 48   **C.** 51   **D.** 56

6. A CD player is on sale for $54.99. The CD player has been discounted 25%. What is the original price of the CD player?

    F. $13.75   **G.** $68.74   **H.** $73.32   **J.** $75.00

7. If $\frac{3}{8} = \frac{x}{32}$, then $x = $ _____.

    A. 4   **B.** 12   **C.** 24   **D.** 96

8. The formula for the area of a triangle is $A = \frac{1}{2}bh$. If the area of a triangle is 48 square feet and the height is 6 feet, what is the length of the base?

    F. 12 feet   **G.** 16 feet   **H.** 24 feet   **J.** 48 feet

9. Juan can buy one ice cream cone for $.90. What is the greatest number of ice cream cones he can buy for $6.00?

    A. 3 cones   **B.** 4 cones   **C.** 5 cones   **D.** 6 cones

10. A train left New York at 1:20 A.M. and reached its stop $3\frac{1}{4}$ hours later. What time did the train reach its stop?

    F. 4:35 A.M.   **G.** 4:45 A.M.   **H.** 5:20 A.M.   **J.** 6:00 A.M.

11. If $\frac{x}{8} = 114$, what is the value of x?

    A. 14.25   **B.** 112   **C.** 812   **D.** 912

Drawing a Picture
Exercises

Draw a diagram to solve each exercise.

1. $\triangle ABC \cong \triangle DEF$. The measure of $\angle A = 51°$, and the measure of $\angle C = 94°$. What is the measure of $\angle E$?

   _____

2. On a bus line, three towns are represented by points G, H, and J. Town G is 55 miles north of Town H, and Town J is 10 mi south of Town G. Which town is between the other two?

   _____

3. The angle bisector of one angle of a triangle measures 42°. The angle bisector of another angle of the triangle measures 36°. What is the measure of the third angle of the triangle?

   _____

4. Team L and Team M have a tug of war. From their starting positions Team L pulls Team M forward 3 meters, and Team L is then pulled forward 5 meters. Team M then pulls Team L forward 4 meters. If the first team to be pulled forward 10 meters loses, how many more meters must Team M pull Team L forward to win?

   _____

5. On a number line point A is 5 units to the left of point B. Point A is located at coordinate -7.2. What is the coordinate of point B?

   _____

6. Circle M has a diameter of 12 inches. Radii $\overline{MN}$ and $\overline{MP}$ form an angle that is not a straight angle. The length of $\overline{NP}$ is *not* 12 inches. Classify $\triangle MNP$ according to its sides.

   _____

7. During a sightseeing tour in Washington D.C., the tour bus travels 4 blocks due north, 6 blocks due east, 12 blocks due south, 22 blocks due west, and 8 blocks due north. At this point, where is the tour bus in relation to its starting point?

   _____

8. How many diagonals can be drawn in a hexagon?

   _____

9. Rectangle $ABCD$ has a perimeter of 62. If the length of $\overline{AD}$ is 14, what is the area of $ABCD$?

   _____

Measuring to Solve

Exercises

Use a ruler to answer each question.

1. The bottom of a soup can is circular, as shown at the right. Measure the radius of the circle in centimeters. Find the circumference of the circle. Use 3.14 for π.

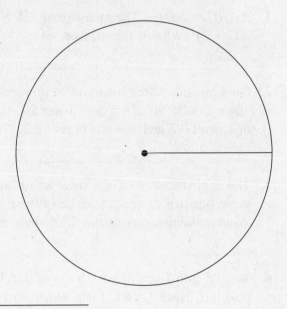

_____

2. The front of a box of cereal is a rectangle, as shown at the right. Measure the dimensions of the rectangle in centimeters. Find the perimeter of the rectangle.

_____

3. A box of tea bags is a cube. The top of the box is the square shown at the right. Measure the dimensions of the square. Find the area of the square.

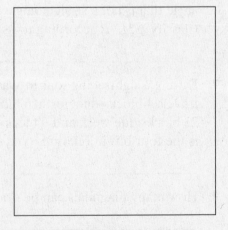

_____

Estimating the Answer

Exercises

Estimate each answer. Circle the letter of the best answer.

1. The circumference of a circle is about 24 ft. Which is closest to the length of the diameter of the circle?

   A. 8 ft   **B.** 9 ft   **C.** 10 ft   **D.** 11 ft

2. Farmer's Merchantile is offering a 30% discount on all farm gates. Which is closest to the discount price of a farm gate that regularly costs $130?

   F. $40   **G.** $90   **H.** $100   **J.** $120

3. The lengths of two legs of a right triangle are 5 ft and 10 ft. Which is closest to the length of the hypotenuse?

   A. 10 ft   **B.** 11 ft   **C.** 13 ft   **D.** 15.5 ft

4. Which is the best estimate for the mean of the data set?
   30, 34, 25, 30, 38, 32

   F. 40   **G.** 35   **H.** 30   **J.** 25

5. You borrow $500 at a 4% simple interest rate. About how much interest will you owe in 2 years?

   A. $20   **B.** $40   **C.** $80   **D.** $520

6. On Friday, $\frac{5}{9}$ of the students at school bought pizza for lunch. About what percent of the students did *not* buy pizza for lunch?

   F. 35%   **G.** 45%   **H.** 55%   **J.** 65%

7. Four pieces of trim, each $8\frac{1}{2}$-inches long are cut from a board 100 inches long. About how many inches of board remain?

   A. 34 inches   **B.** 50 inches   **C.** 66 inches   **D.** 75 inches

8. Linden bought a jacket for 15% off the regular retail price of $110. What did Linden pay for the jacket?

   F. $16.50   **G.** $65.60   **H.** $75.80   **J.** $93.50

Answering the Question Asked

Exercises

Use the table below to answer exercises 1–4.

Record Breakers

What	Name	Size
Deepest Lake	Baikal	5,315 feet deep
Largest Continent	Asia	17,212,041 square miles
Lowest Land Point	Dead Sea	1,349 feet below sea level
Largest Gorge	Grand Canyon	277 miles long, up to 18 miles wide, 1 mile deep
Longest Mountain Range	Andes	more than 5,000 miles
Longest River	Nile	4,145 miles
Shortest River	Roe	201 feet

1. What is the longest river?

   A. Nile   **B.** Roe   **C.** Andes   **D.** Baikal

2. What is the difference between the longest and shortest river, in feet?

   F. 3,944 feet   **G.** 4,346 feet   **H.** 2,189 feet   **J.** 2.189×10^7 feet

3. At its widest point, what is the volume of the Grand Canyon?

   A. 4,986 miles^3 **B.** 3,256 miles^3 **C.** 296 miles^3 **D.** 295 miles^3

4. What is the difference in length between the longest mountain range and the longest river?

   F. 300 miles   **G.** 855 miles   **H.** 1,000 miles   **J.** 2,290 miles

Use the double bar graph for exercises 5–7.

5. Which of the following continents had the least amount of change in wheat production per 1,000 capita between 1961 and 2000?

   A. Africa   **B.** Asia

   C. North America   **D.** South America

6. What is the approximate change in Europe's wheat production per 1,000 capita from 1961 to 2000?

   F. 100 tons   **G.** 150 tons

   H. 170 tons   **J.** 200 tons

7. In 2000, what is the approximate mean of wheat produced for all continents shown?

   A. 200 tons   **B.** 250 tons

   C. 300 tons   **D.** 350 tons

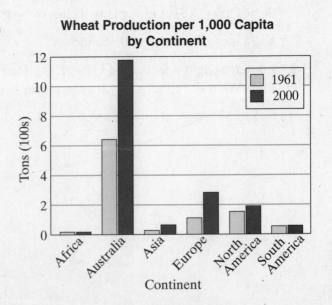

Wheat Production per 1,000 Capita by Continent

Interpreting Data

Exercises

Use the graphs at the right to answer each question.

1. What is the median of the scores shown in the stem-and-leaf plot at the right?

   A. 6   **B.** 8   **C.** 81   **D.** 86

2. What is the range of the scores shown in the stem-and-leaf plot at the right?

   F. 9   **G.** 23   **H.** 31   **J.** 86

3. Which statement is best supported by the information in the bar graph at the right?

   A. More girls voted for "Pandas" than voted for "Tigers."

   B. The total number of votes for "Pandas" was the same as the total number of votes for "Dragons."

   C. The same number of girls voted for "Dragons" as voted for "Tigers."

   D. The fewest number of votes went to "Tigers."

4. Which statement is NOT supported by the information in the line graph at the right?

   F. It took Riley approximately 40 minutes to drive to work.

   G. Riley's maximum speed on the way to work is about 58 miles per hour.

   H. Riley stops 4 times on his way to work.

   J. Riley's maximum speed for the first 10 minutes of the drive is about 20 miles per hour.

Scores on Science Test

```
9 | 0 0 1 3 5 7 7 8
8 | 0 1 1 1 2 3 6 8 8 9
7 | 6 8 8 9
6 | 7
```

Key: 9 | 0 means 90

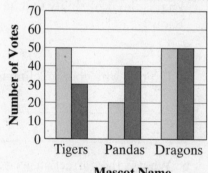

Votes for New Mascot Name

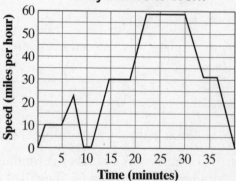

Riley's Drive to Work

Eliminating Answers

Exercises

Solve each problem.

1. A quality-control inspector found 40 defective crayons out of 1,000 that she checked. What percent of the crayons were defective?

   A. 400%   **B.** 100%   **C.** 40%   **D.** 4%

   a. Explain why you can eliminate answer choices A and C.

   _____

   b. What is the correct answer choice? _____

2. A bag contains 6 green apples, 8 red apples, and 16 yellow apples. What is the probability that an apple selected at random is yellow?

   F. $\frac{1}{8}$ **G.** $\frac{4}{15}$ **H.** $\frac{8}{15}$ **J.** 1

   a. Explain why you can eliminate answer choices F and J.

   _____

   _____

   b. What is the correct answer choice? _____

3. At a carnival you have the chance to spin the letter wheel. The letter wheel has 26 spaces, each with a different letter of the alphabet. You spin the spinner twice. Find $P(C$, then $H)$.

   A. $\frac{1}{2}$ **B.** $\frac{1}{26}$ **C.** $\frac{1}{52}$ **D.** $\frac{1}{676}$

   a. Explain why you can eliminate answer choices A and B.

   _____

   _____

   b. What is the correct answer choice? _____

4. How many three-number permutations can be formed from the numbers 1, 2, 3, 4, and 5, if no digit is used more than once?

   F. 240   **G.** 120   **H.** 60   **J.** 30

   a. Explain why you can eliminate answer choices F and G.

   _____

   _____

   b. What is the correct answer choice? _____

Name_____ Class_____ Date_____

NAEP Practice Test

1. Lindsay needs to buy 12 cans of tomato sauce to make spaghetti for her family. Each can of spaghetti sauce costs $0.89. Which expression gives Lindsay the most accurate estimation of the total cost of 12 cans?

   A $2 × 12

   B $1 × 12

   C $0.75 × 12

   D $0.50 × 12

   E $0.25 × 12

2. Between which two consecutive whole numbers does $\sqrt{58}$ lie?

   A 4 and 5

   B 5 and 6

   C 6 and 7

   D 7 and 8

   E 8 and 9

3. Jill is going to run a 5 kilometer race. If 1 kilometer is approximately $\frac{5}{8}$ mile, how many miles long is the race?

   A $2\frac{1}{2}$ miles

   B 3 miles

   C $3\frac{1}{8}$ miles

   D 5 miles

   E 8 miles

4. At the football team's end of the year banquet, there were five pies to choose from for dessert. The shaded region of each circle shows how much pie was left over. Which pie had the most left over?

   A   B

   C   D

   E

5. Which data set has the median with the greatest value?

   A 2, 3, 2, 3, 7, 7, 5, 6, 3

   B 2, 2, 3, 2, 4, 7, 5, 6, 6

   C 3, 3, 2, 6, 7, 6, 7, 7, 4

   D 3, 4, 6, 3, 2, 7, 5, 6, 5

   E 4, 3, 4, 7, 3, 4, 6, 5, 2

6. Jack's last six test scores are 75, 78, 83, 80, 79, and 84. If he scores a 90 on the next test, by how much will his mean test score increase? Round to the nearest hundredth.

   A 1.45

   B 8.30

   C 14.50

   D 79.80

   E 81.30

7. Jerry has 3 less than 4 times as many baseball cards as his little brother. Which expression represents the number of baseball cards Jerry has?

A v

B $7v$

C $3v - 7$

D $4v - 3$

E $3v - 4$

8. What is the value of the expression $ab^2 + 3(a - b)$ if $a = 3$ and $b = -2$?

A 3

B 13

C 27

D 37

E 51

9. There are 192 people going on a field trip to the museum. If one bus seats 32 people, which equation can be used to find the number of buses needed for the trip?

A $32x = 192$

B $192x = 32$

C $32 + x = 192$

D $\frac{x}{192} = 32$

E $\frac{x}{32} = 192$

10. Solve for w.

$$w - 3 = -8$$

A -11

B -5

C $2\frac{2}{3}$

D 11

E 24

11. Jim and Beth are trying to solve the equation $7 - x = 25$. Jim says that if they just subtract 7 from both sides, they will be finished. What should Beth say to Jim to prove him wrong?

A No, what we need to do is add 7 to both sides.

B No, what we need to do is add x to both sides.

C No, we should add 7 to both sides and then divide both sides by -1.

D No, we should subtract 7 from both sides and then divide both sides by -1.

E No, we should add x to both sides and then add 7 to both sides.

12. Solve for x.

$$3x + 6 = 7$$

A -3

B $-\frac{1}{3}$

C $\frac{1}{3}$

D 3

E $4\frac{1}{3}$

GO ON

13. Which equation represents the model?

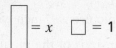

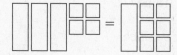

A $7x = 7$

B $3x + 4 = 7$

C $4x + 3 = 6x + 1$

D $3x - 4 = x - 6$

E $3x + 4 = x + 6$

14. Which inequality represents the graph?

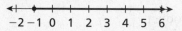

A $x > -1$

B $x \geq -1$

C $x < -1$

D $x \leq -1$

E $x = -1$

15. Which of the following is NOT a solution for the inequality $r - 8 > 16$?

A 24

B 25

C 26

D 27

E 28

16. If $\dfrac{x}{-6} \leq 12$, then

A $x \leq -72$.

B $x \geq -72$.

C $x \leq -2$.

D $x \geq -2$.

E $x \leq 72$.

17. The table lists the distance from each planet to the Sun. What is the distance between the two planets that are furthest from the Sun?

Planet	Distance from Sun (in kilometers)
Saturn	1.49×10^8 km
Neptune	4.50×10^9 km
Venus	1.08×10^8 km
Jupiter	7.78×10^8 km
Uranus	2.87×10^9 km

A 7.37×10^9 km

B 1.63×10^8 km

C 3.28×10^7 km

D 1.70×10^{10} km

E 1.63×10^9 km

18. Hilary is making holiday gift bags for all the children she baby-sits. She has 126 toys. Of the choices listed below, what is the most bags she can make if each bag has an equal number of toys in it?

A 2

B 3

C 5

D 9

E 10

19. What is the largest prime factor of 924?

   A 2

   B 3

   C 4

   D 7

   E 11

20. Which fraction, when simplified, does NOT equal $\frac{2}{3}$?

   A $\frac{4}{6}$

   B $\frac{10}{15}$

   C $\frac{18}{20}$

   D $\frac{24}{36}$

   E $\frac{30}{45}$

21. An earthworm moves $\frac{5}{8}$ inch one minute and $\frac{3}{4}$ inch the next minute. What is the total distance the earthworm traveled in these two minutes?

   A $\frac{1}{2}$ inch

   B $\frac{8}{12}$ inch

   C 1 inch

   D $1\frac{1}{12}$ inch

   E $1\frac{3}{8}$ inch

22. A picture measures $5\frac{1}{8}$ inch by $10\frac{1}{4}$ inch. The frame for the picture is $\frac{3}{4}$ inch wide. What are the dimensions of the picture, including the frame?

   A $7\frac{3}{8}$ inch by $9\frac{1}{2}$ inch

   B $6\frac{5}{8}$ inch by $11\frac{3}{4}$ inch

   C $6\frac{1}{4}$ inch by $11\frac{3}{4}$ inch

   D $4\frac{1}{8}$ inch by $10\frac{1}{4}$ inch

   E $5\frac{1}{8}$ inch by $9\frac{1}{4}$ inch

23. Find the product. $\frac{5}{8} \times \frac{6}{7} \times 1\frac{1}{3}$

   A $\frac{5}{28}$

   B $\frac{45}{112}$

   C $\frac{5}{7}$

   D $\frac{15}{28}$

   E $1\frac{2}{5}$

24. Find the quotient. $4\frac{1}{5} \div 1\frac{2}{5}$

   A $1\frac{1}{5}$

   B $1\frac{3}{5}$

   C 3

   D 4

   E $5\frac{22}{25}$

25. Harry is measuring the width of the street in front of his house. Which unit of measurement should be used?

A millimeters

B inches

C meters

D miles

E kilometers

26. On the first day of a hike, Mary hiked 3.25 kilometers. On the second day, she hiked 2.1 kilometers. What is the best estimate, to the nearest whole kilometer, of the total distance that Mary hiked?

A 1.05 km

B 5 km

C 5.55 km

D 5.6 km

E 6 km

27. Which figure has the largest *shaded* area to *non-shaded* area ratio?

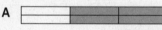
A

B

C

D

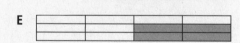
E

28. A train can travel 147 miles in 3 hours. How many miles can the train travel in 1 hour?

A 43 miles

B 49 miles

C 50 miles

D 57 miles

E 441 miles

29. Mr. Carlson is grading quizzes on solving proportions. Which response correctly used cross products to solve the proportion $\frac{15}{x} = \frac{6}{4}$?

A $15 = 6x$

B $15 = 24x$

C $(6)(4) = 15x$

D $(15)(4) = 6x$

E $(6)(15) = 4x$

30. If $\frac{16}{21} = \frac{x}{14}$, then $x =$

A $10\frac{2}{3}$.

B $18\frac{3}{8}$.

C 24.

D 32.

E 42.

GO ON

31. A tree with a height of 8-ft has a shadow 6-ft long. At the same time of day, a nearby building has a 16-ft shadow. How tall is the building?

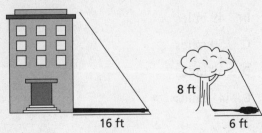

16 ft   8 ft   6 ft

A 3 ft

B 12 ft

C $21\frac{1}{3}$ ft

D $24\frac{2}{3}$ ft

E 32 ft

32. The model car below has a scale of $1 \text{ inch} = 2\frac{1}{2}$ feet. What is the length of the actual car?

6 in.

A 2.4 ft

B 4.5 ft

C 8.5 ft

D 15.0 ft

E 16.0 ft

33. An architect is drawing a blueprint of a house that is being remodeled. The scale is 1 cm = 1.5 m. If the dimensions of the actual kitchen are 9 m × 6 m, what is the area of the kitchen on the blueprint?

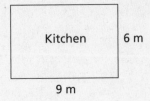

Kitchen   6 m

9 m

A 12 cm^2

B 18 cm^2

C 24 cm^2

D 27 cm^2

E 54 cm^2

34. Annie bought the items below and received a 25% discount off the regular price of each item. The sales tax in Annie's state is 6.5%. What is the total that Annie paid for these items, including sales tax?

$45.99 $15.99

$32.99

A $23.74

B $71.23

C $75.86

D $94.97

E $126.43

GO ON

35. Kory scored 36 points out of a possible 40 points. What percent of the possible points did Kory score?

A   5%

B   35%

C   70%

D   90%

E   142%

36. Eight hundred students ride the bus to school. This is 25% of the school's student population. How many students attend the school?

A   200

B   1,000

C   1,800

D   3,200

E   3,800

37. A store manager buys leather wallets for $12 and then marks the price up 250%. How much does the manager sell the wallets for?

A $30

B $42

C $60

D $250

E $262

38. In which figure is the measure of $\angle CBD$ equal to 45°?

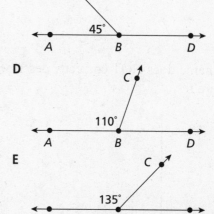
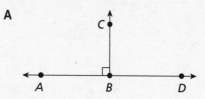
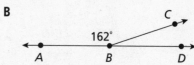
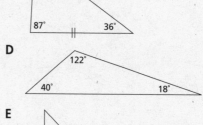
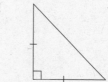

39. Which triangle is a right isosceles triangle?

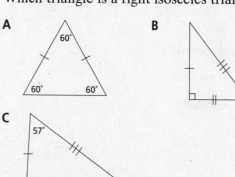

40. What is the measure of $\angle F$?

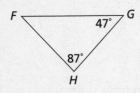

- **A** 24°
- **B** 46°
- **C** 47°
- **D** 90°
- **E** 134°

41. Which name does NOT correctly describe the figure?

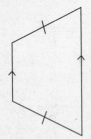

- **A** quadrilateral
- **B** polygon
- **C** trapezoid
- **D** rhombus
- **E** isosceles

42. Which polygon has four congruent sides, no right angles, and opposite sides parallel?

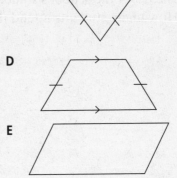

43. A square can be classified as all of the following except:

- **A** a polygon.
- **B** a triangle.
- **C** a rectangle.
- **D** a rhombus.
- **E** a quadrilateral.

Name _____ Class _____ Date _____

44. What is the sum of the angle measures of the figure?

A 180°

B 360°

C 540°

D 720°

E 900°

45. What is *DE*, to the nearest tenth of a centimeter?

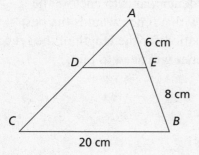

A 8.6 cm

B 10.2 cm

C 15.0 cm

D 18.0 cm

E 26.7 cm

46. What is the radius of circle *P*?

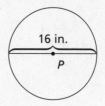

A 4 inches

B 8 inches

C 16 inches

D 20 inches

E 24 inches

47. If 200 students participate in extra-curricular activities, how many play football?

Student Participation in Extracurricular Activities

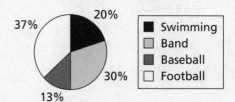

A 26 students

B 40 students

C 60 students

D 74 students

E 120 students

GO ON

48. Which figure has the smallest area?

A

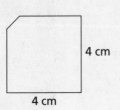

4 cm

4 cm

B

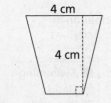

4 cm

4 cm

C

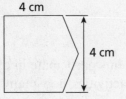

4 cm

4 cm

D

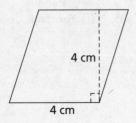

4 cm

4 cm

E

4 cm

4 cm

49. A child is using sidewalk chalk to draw a triangular-shaped area for a game. If the height of the area is twice the base, and the base is 6 feet, what is the area of the game?

A   12 ft²

B   36 ft²

C   72 ft²

D   84 ft²

E   120 ft²

50. A parcel of land is for sale. It is priced at $100 per square foot. Use the figure shown to find the cost of the entire piece of land.

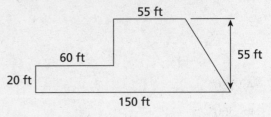

55 ft

60 ft

55 ft

20 ft

150 ft

A $518.75

B $1050.50

C $5187.50

D $39,500.00

E $518,750.00

51. A circular fountain has a radius of 10 feet. If the gardener wants to enclose the fountain with a fence, what is the best approximation for the length of the fence the gardener will need to buy?

A   20 feet

B   36 feet

C   63 feet

D   100 feet

E   314 feet

52. A boat's sail is 6 meters long and 8 meters high. What is the length of the diagonal of the sail?

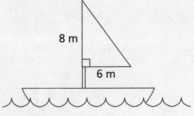

8 m

6 m

A   10 meters

B   13 meters

C   25 meters

D   100 meters

E   121 meters

53. A silo has a diameter of 3 meters and a height of 8 meters. Approximately, how much grain does the silo hold?

  A 38 m^3

  B 57 m^3

  C 75 m^3

  D 153 m^3

  E 226 m^3

54. If the pattern in the list below continues, what will be the next number after 31?

$16, 23, 20, 27, 24, 31, \ldots$

  A 25

  B 28

  C 33

  D 38

  E 41

55. Which operation should you use to get the next number in the pattern?

$8, 11, 14, 17, \ldots$

  A Take the square root.

  B Multiply by 3.

  C Add 3.

  D Subtract 3.

  E Divide by 3.

56. Which rule represents the graph of the points shown on the coordinate plane?

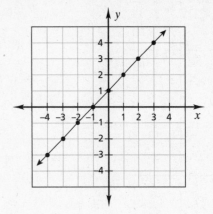

  A $y = -x$

  B $y = x - 1$

  C $y = x + 1$

  D $y = -x - 1$

  E $y = -x + 1$

57. Which of the following ordered pairs is a solution of the equation $3x - 4y = 12$?

  A $(4, 6)$

  B $(3, 4)$

  C $(0, 3)$

  D $(-4, 0)$

  E $(-4, -6)$

58. The line passing through which two pair of points has the steepest slope?

  A $(1, 2)$ and $(5, -2)$

  B $(2, -4)$ and $(3, 0)$

  C $(2, 5)$ and $(-3, 6)$

  D $(-2, 1)$ and $(5, 6)$

  E $(-1, 2)$ and $(0, 4)$

$\boxed{\text{GO ON} \Rightarrow}$

59. Which is a graph of a linear function?

A
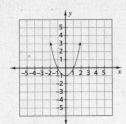

B
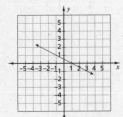

C
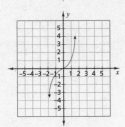

D
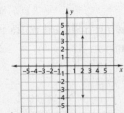

E
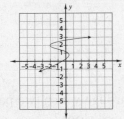

60. What type of trend would you expect to see in a scatter plot comparing a person's height and eye color?

A positive

B negative

C opposite

D none

E inverse

61. You are conducting a survey on a new school color. Which method will give you a random sample?

A Survey all students whose name you pull out of a hat.

B Survey all students who drive a red or blue car.

C Survey all students with a grade point average of 3.5 or better.

D Survey all eighth grade cheerleaders.

E Survey the teachers in the teacher's lounge.

62. A bottle contains 6 red marbles, 9 blue marbles, 3 green marbles, 8 yellow marbles, and 4 white marbles. Which event has the greatest probability?

A P(choosing a blue marble)

B P(choosing a red or green marble)

C P(choosing a yellow or blue marble)

D P(choosing a white or green marble)

E P(choosing a red or white marble)

63. Ray rolled a number cube 10 times and got the following numbers, 2, 2, 3, 3, 1, 5, 6, 6, 6, 2. What is the difference between the experimental probability of rolling a 6 and the theoretical probability of rolling a 6?

A $\frac{1}{10}$

B $\frac{1}{6}$

C $\frac{2}{15}$

D $\frac{3}{10}$

E $\frac{1}{2}$

Short Constructed Response

64. Describe two ways to find the 15th term of the sequence shown below.
Which of these ways would be easier to use if you were to find the
100th term of the sequence? Explain your reasoning.

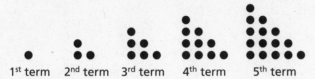

1st term   2nd term   3rd term   4th term   5th term

65. Mary planned to spend 20 minutes on the treadmill today at the gym. She
spent 5 minutes warming up by walking and then 2 minutes increasing her
rate constantly until she was at a full run. She then ran for 6 minutes.
At this point the electricity turned off and Mary had to stop instantly. Create
a graph that shows how Mary's rate changed throughout the time she was on
the treadmill. Explain your reasoning.

66. The president of a sugar company has to choose the least expensive of three
different containers in which to package 1,000 cubic centimeters of sugar. It
costs $0.50 per square centimeter to make any of the three containers shown
below. Which container should the president choose? Why?

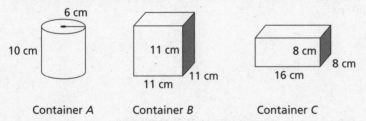

Container *A*   Container *B*   Container *C*

GO ON

Extended Constructed Response

67. You want to enclose a garden in your backyard with segments of fence that are all the same length. The dimensions of the garden are shown below.

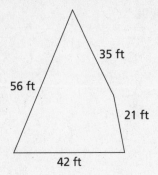

What is the greatest length that a segment of fence can be so that the segments will fill each side without gaps?

If you use segments with the length you found above, how many segments are needed to enclose the entire garden?

68. Every student in the school had three days to vote for their favorite school mascot. The school newspaper published the following bar graph to show how many students liked each of the four different school mascots.

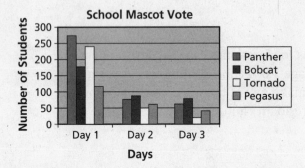

Which mascot should the school choose? Explain.

69. Janell knows that $x < y$ and that $x > 0$ and $y > 0$. She claims that this means that $x^2 < y^2$. Is she correct? Why or why not?

70. Peter travels 90 miles due north and then 60 miles due east to arrive at his grandmother's house. His car gets 25 miles per gallon and he pays $1.12 per gallon of gasoline. Make a diagram of the route Peter travels to his grandmother's house. On your diagram, draw the shortest possible route. If Peter could use the shortest possible route, how much money would he save on gasoline? Explain your answer.

SAT 10 Practice Test

· ·

PS *Mathematics: Problem Solving*

Read each question. Then mark your answer on the answer sheet.

1. **Which of these numbers is the coordinate of point Q?**

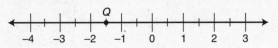

   A $\frac{1}{2}$

   B $-\frac{1}{2}$

   C $-1\frac{1}{2}$

   D $-1\frac{3}{4}$

2. **Which of these is less than −1.85 but greater than −2?**

   F −1.9

   G −1.8

   H $-1\frac{1}{2}$

   J 1.7

3. **A jeweler sells gold chains that are $\frac{3}{16}$ in., $\frac{1}{8}$ in., $\frac{2}{4}$ in., and $\frac{5}{8}$ in. thick. Which of the following shows these sizes in correct order from smallest to largest?**

   A $\frac{2}{4}$ in., $\frac{1}{8}$ in., $\frac{5}{8}$ in., $\frac{3}{16}$ in.

   B $\frac{1}{4}$ in., $\frac{3}{16}$ in., $\frac{2}{4}$ in., $\frac{5}{8}$ in.

   C $\frac{3}{16}$ in., $\frac{1}{8}$ in., $\frac{5}{8}$ in., $\frac{2}{4}$ in.

   D $\frac{1}{8}$ in., $\frac{3}{16}$ in., $\frac{2}{4}$ in., $\frac{5}{8}$ in.

4. **Odetta found the inside diameter of a tube. She measured the diameter as 0.125 in. What is another way of expressing the length of the diameter?**

   F $\frac{1}{125}$ in.

   G $\frac{1}{12}$ in.

   H $\frac{1}{8}$ in.

   J $\frac{1}{4}$ in.

5. **Which fraction is equivalent to $\frac{36}{45}$ and in lowest terms?**

   A $\frac{4}{9}$

   B $\frac{12}{15}$

   C $\frac{4}{5}$

   D $\frac{11}{5}$

6. **Which of these does NOT have the same value as $1\frac{2}{5}$?**

   F 1.4

   G $\frac{7}{5}$

   H 1.40

   J 1.25

>**GO ON**

· ·

7. Which of these is a factor of 1,055?

A 75

B 105

C 201

D 211

8. Janine knows the area of the base of a prism is 19 yd^2. The height of the prism is 20.8 yd. Which of the following is the best estimate of the capacity of the prism?

F 200 yd^3

G 300 yd^3

H 350 yd^3

J 400 yd^3

9. The area of a circle with a radius of 2.6 cm is about 21.2264 cm^2. To which place value is the area expressed?

A Hundred thousandths

B Ten thousandths

C Thousandths

D Hundredths

10. The mean distance of the sun from Earth is 1.5×10^8 kilometers. Which of the following shows the number in standard from?

F 15,000,000

G 150,000,000

H 1,500,000,000

J 15,000,000,000

11. Which is the solution of $3x + 4 = -11$?

A $x = -45$

B $x = -15$

C $x = -5$

D $x = -2\frac{1}{3}$

12. Which expression is equivalent to $4 \times 5\frac{1}{2}$?

F $4\left(5 + \frac{1}{2}\right)$

G $20\frac{1}{2}$

H $4\left(5 \times \frac{1}{2}\right)$

J $4 + \left(5 \times \frac{1}{2}\right)$

13. Mr. Herold repairs dishwashers. He charges $25 for a house call that is more than 30 miles from his shop plus $20 per hour. If h represents the hours he must work on a machine 45 miles from his shop, which of the following expressions could be used to find his fee?

A $20h$

B $25h + 20$

C $20h + 25$

D $60h$

```
GO ON
```

PS SAT 10 Practice Test

14. What is the value of $4a + 2a - b$ if $a = 3$ and $b = 4$?

F 9

G 10

H 14

J 17

15. This graph shows the Ramirez family budget. Which expenses together make up less than 25% of the budget?

Ramirez Family Budget

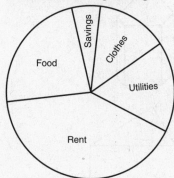

A Savings and rent

B Savings and clothes

C Food and rent

D Food and clothes

16. Find the missing output value for this table.

Input	1	2	10	5
Output	5	9	41	?

F 10

G 12

H 20

J 21

17. What is the tenth term in the pattern given below?

$-1, 1, 3, 5, \ldots$

A 17

B 16

C 15

D 14

18. A recipe for fruit punch mixes 2 L of orange juice, 3 L of pineapple juice, and 1 L of seltzer. How many liters of orange juice will be needed if 18 L of pineapple juice are used?

F 18 L

G 12 L

H 9 L

J 6 L

19. The results of a survey showed that 80% of the people surveyed planned to vote for the town referendum to improve the town's street lights. If 200 people were part of the survey, how many were planning to vote for this improvement?

A 40 people

B 160 people

C 180 people

D 200 people

GO ON

20. A letter is chosen at random from the word MISSISSIPPI. What is the probability that the chosen letter is an S?

F $\frac{1}{11}$

G $\frac{1}{4}$

H $\frac{4}{11}$

J $\frac{4}{7}$

21. Classify ∠*BEC*.

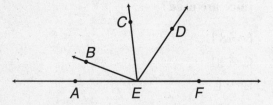

A Straight

B Obtuse

C Right

D Acute

22. Luke wants to classify these polyhedrons. Which polyhedron is not a prism?

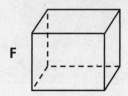

F

G

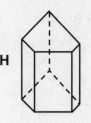

H

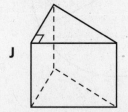

J

PS SAT 10 Practice Test

23. This line graph shows the temperature in the lobby and on the 15th floor of an office building during several different times of the day. What is the greatest difference between the temperatures in the two floors at any given time?

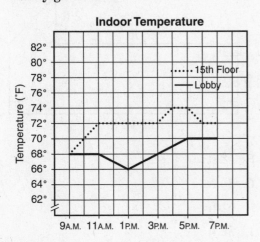

Indoor Temperature

A 10°F

B 8°F

C 6°F

D 4°F

24. This table shows the amount of cereal that is packed into small boxes of granola.

Boxes of Cereal	Number of Grams (g)
1	400 g
2	800 g
3	1200 g
4	1600 g

If this pattern continues, how many grams of cereal would there be in 9 boxes?

F 3000 g

G 3200 g

H 3600 g

J 4200 g

25. Maurice recorded the number of hours he worked in each of the past five weeks: 32.5, 40.5, 37.75, 20.0, and 31.5. What is the mean number of hours per week worked over the five-week period?

A 30.75 hours

B 32.45 hours

C 32.6 hours

D 33 hours

26. This chart shows the results of spinning a blue, red, and white spinner.

Spins	Tally
Blue	IIII IIII
Red	IIII IIII IIII
White	II

How many spins were there in all?

F 10 spins

G 22 spins

H 24 spins

J 26 spins

27. Tyrone has seven books on his desk between bookends. In how many different ways can he arrange the books from left to right?

A 14 ways

B 49 ways

C 720 ways

D 5040 ways

GO ON

28. Which of the following is a radius of circle *O*?

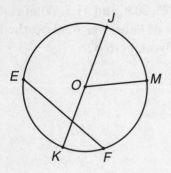

F *O*

G $\overline{OM}$

H $\overline{EF}$

J $\overline{JK}$

29. Use the figure.

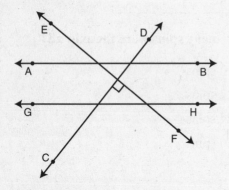

Which of these is true?

A $\overleftrightarrow{AB}$ and $\overleftrightarrow{CD}$ are perpendicular.

B $\overleftrightarrow{EF}$ and $\overleftrightarrow{AB}$ are perpendicular.

C $\overleftrightarrow{CD}$ and $\overleftrightarrow{EF}$ are perpendicular.

D $\overleftrightarrow{GH}$ and $\overleftrightarrow{AB}$ are perpendicular.

30. John wants a garden that is at least 64 square feet. His friend sketched a garden design as shown below. How many more square feet does the garden have to be in order to meet John's area requirements?

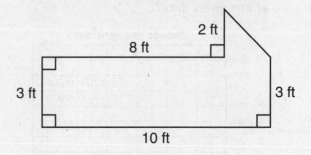

F 25 ft²

G 30 ft²

H 32 ft²

J 52 ft²

31. To the nearest hundredth, what is the circumference of the circle?

Use *C* = *πd* and *π* ≈ 3.14.

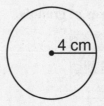

A 12.56 cm

B 25.12 cm

C 50.24 cm

D 97.21 cm

PS SAT 10 Practice Test

32. The aquarium is a rectangular prism with dimensions 30 in. by 20 in. by 16 in. Estimate the maximum volume of water it can hold.

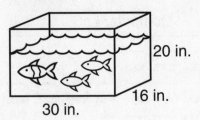

F 960 in^3

G 4800 in^3

H 9000 in^3

J 18,000 in^3

33. Triangle ABC is moved to form triangle $A'B'C'$. What is the best description of this transformation?

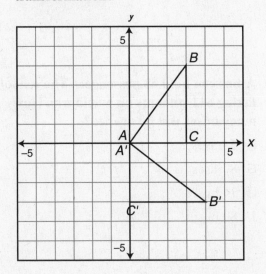

A A translation 4 units down

B A reflection across the x-axis

C A clockwise rotation of 90°

D A clockwish rotation of 180°

34. Triangle ABC is a right triangle. The coordinates of A are $(-2, 1)$ and the coordinates of B are $(3, 1)$. Which of the following could be the coordinates of C?

F $(3, 5)$

G $(5, -1)$

H $(2, 4)$

J $(-1, 3)$

35. A cable is 78 m long. Workers cut it into 30 pieces of equal length. How many millimeters long is each piece?

A 26 mm

B 260 mm

C 2600 mm

D 26,000 mm

36. Use the centimeter ruler. Find the perimeter of rectangle $PQRS$.

F 10 cm

G 20 cm

H 24 cm

J 40 cm

GO ON

37. Ralph left home at 7:25 A.M. He returned home at 9:08 P.M. What was the elapsed time?

A 1 hr 43 min

B 13 hr 43 min

C 13 hr 83 min

D 14 hr 23 min

38. Triangle *ABC* is similar to triangle *DEF*. Find the length of *x*.

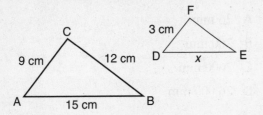

F 3 cm

G 4 cm

H 5 cm

J 6 cm

39. A scale drawing shows the plan for a computer lab. The length of the longest wall on the drawing is $3\frac{1}{4}$ in. What is the actual length of the wall in feet?

Computer Lab

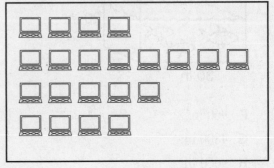

$\frac{1}{4}$ in. = 2 ft

A 8 ft

B 24 cm

C 26 ft

D 28 ft

40. A bus can hold 48 passengers. The school is taking 632 students on a field trip. How many buses will be needed?

F 5 buses

G 8 buses

H 14 buses

J 80 buses

PS SAT 10 Practice Test

41. Alice is remodeling her home. She has remodeling bills for the following amounts: $834, $792, $810, and $795. Which of these is the best estimate of the cost of her remodeling?

A $2800

B $3200

C $4000

D $4800

42. Which of these is the best estimate of the area of the figure below?

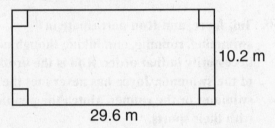

10.2 m

29.6 m

F 270 m^2

G 279 m2

H 300 m^2

J 310 m^2

43. Tamara received a 5% wage increase. She earns $198 a week. Estimate how much of a weekly wage increase she received.

A $5

B $10

C $20

D $100

44. Darrel finds two pieces of wire that measure $\frac{7}{12}$ in. and $\frac{7}{8}$ in. Estimate the total length of the two pieces of wire together.

F $\frac{1}{2}$ in.

G 1 in.

H $1\frac{1}{2}$ in.

J 2 in.

45. Liz is buying tubes of oil paint at an art supply store. Each tube of paint costs between $2 and $3. What is a reasonable cost for 12 tubes of paint?

A $20

B $30

C $38

D $40

GO ON

46. This table lists the cost of tickets to the state fair. On Saturday, 503 tickets were sold. What information do you need to find out how much money was collected on Saturday?

State Fair Tickets	
Adult	$8
Child	$3

F The price of a ticket

G The number of tickets sold on Sunday

H The number of adult tickets sold on Saturday

J The number of senior citizens who attended on Saturday

47. Jan opened a box of computer disks. She gave half of the disks to her brother. She gave her friend Lisa 5 disks. She put 10 disks in her school bag. Then Jan had 5 disks left in the box. How many disks were in the box when she first opened it?

A 40 disks

B 30 disks

C 20 disks

D 10 disks

48. Keri studied for 95 minutes. She studied math 6 minutes longer than she studied science. She studied history 8 minutes longer than she studied math. How long did she study science?

F 20 minutes

G 25 minutes

H 30 minutes

J 35 minutes

49. A community center uses a phone tree to tell members important information. The center leader makes 2 calls to start the phone tree. Then each person who gets a call makes 2 calls. So on the second round, 4 calls are made. On the third round 8 calls are made. How many calls are made on the fifth round?

A 32 calls

B 24 calls

C 16 calls

D 12 calls

50. Tai, Joyce, and Ron participate in swimming, running, and hiking though not necessarily in that order. Ron is the brother of the swimmer. Joyce has never met the swimmer or the runner. Match the people with their sports.

F Tai is the runner, Joyce is the swimmer, and Ron is the hiker.

G Tai is the hiker, Joyce is the runner, and Ron is the swimmer.

H Tai is the runner, Joyce is the hiker, and Ron is the swimmer.

J Tai is the swimmer, Joyce is the hiker, and Ron is the runner.

SAT 10 Practice Test

 Mathematics: Procedures

Find each answer. Then mark the space on your answer sheet. If a correct answer is not here, mark the space for NH.

1.   39
   × 34

  A 1126

  B 1296

  C 1316

  D 1446

  E NH

2.   740
   × 29

  F 20,460

  G 21,460

  H 22,360

  J 22,870

  K NH

3. 25)5245

  A $29\frac{4}{5}$

  B $209\frac{4}{5}$

  C $290\frac{4}{5}$

  D $299\frac{4}{5}$

  E NH

4. 12.23 × 0.4 =

  F 489.2

  G 48.92

  H 4.892

  J 0.4892

  K NH

5. $1\frac{5}{13} + 3\frac{9}{13} =$

  A $4\frac{1}{13}$

  B $4\frac{7}{13}$

  C $5\frac{1}{13}$

  D $5\frac{7}{13}$

  E NH

6. $\frac{2}{3} \times \frac{9}{5} =$

  F $2\frac{7}{10}$

  G $1\frac{3}{5}$

  H $1\frac{1}{5}$

  J $\frac{10}{27}$

  K NH

7. 1.4)0.84

  A 60

  B 6.0

  C 0.6

  D 0.06

  E NH

GO ON

SAT 10 Practice Test

8. $8\frac{5}{9} - 5\frac{7}{9} =$

F $\frac{7}{9}$

G $2\frac{7}{9}$

H $3\frac{2}{9}$

J $3\frac{7}{9}$

K NH

9. The distance from the house to the garage is 120 feet. Telephone wire is sold by the yard. How many yards should Mr. Lewis buy if he wants enough wire to reach from the house to the garage?

A 10 yd

B 40 yd

C 60 yd

D 80 yd

E NH

10. Allie reviewed her company's travel mileage for the past four months. What was the company's total mileage for these months?

Month	Total Mileage
April	17,281
May	5,326
June	42,381
July	2,580

F 66,568 mi

G 67,568 mi

H 67,668 mi

J 68,468 mi

K NH

11. An artist pours 1700 cm³ of plaster into a mold to make a prism. She has 7000 cm³ of plaster. How many times can she completely fill the mold?

A 4

B 5

C 30

D 41

E NH

12. Laura and Bert sold tickets to the school play. Each ticket costs $6. Laura sold 7 tickets. Bert sold 5 tickets. How much money in all should Laura and Bert have collected?

F $72

G $42

H $30

J $12

K NH

13. Jamal has the following scores on his math tests: 85, 92, 79, 94, and 100. What is the average (mean) of his test scores?

A 21

B 75

C 90

D 92

E NH

GO ON

SAT 10 Practice Test

14. Miko has $2486 in her checking account. She wants to write a check for $3291. How much does she need to deposit before writing the check?

   F $705

   G $803

   H $820

   J $825

   K NH

15. A rectangular field has a perimeter of 13.34 km. The width of the field is 2.17 km. What is the length of the field?

   A 11.17 km

   B 9 km

   C 4.5 km

   D 2.25 km

   E NH

16. This year 4% of the people in a village do not have a television set. If 250 people do not have a television set, how many people live in the village?

   F 6250 people

   G 1000 people

   H 62.5 people

   J 31 people

   K NH

17. Samantha bought three magazines for $2.95 each and two cards for $1.86 each. How much did she spend?

   A $23.68

   B $12.47

   C $11.57

   D $10.68

   E NH

18. At the EZ Market, apples are usually $1.29 lb. This week they are on sale for $0.99 lb. How much will Ms. Sanchez save if she buys 5 pounds of apples this week?

   F $0.30

   G $1.50

   H $4.95

   J $5.19

   K NH

19.

Port St. Lucie, Florida	Population
2000	89,000
1990	55,761
1980	14,690

How many more people lived in Port St. Lucie in 1990 than in 1980?

   A 70,451 people

   B 41,071 people

   C 39,280 people

   D 30,690 people

   E NH

20. Mr. Lammers bought $4\frac{3}{4}$ yd of felt at $4 per yd. How much did he spend on felt in all?

F $16.75

G $19.00

H $20.00

J $28.00

K NH

21. A bolt of fabric contains 30 yards of material. How much material remains on the bolt once you cut off a $5\frac{1}{4}$-yard piece of fabric?

A $1\frac{2}{4}$ yd

B $5\frac{1}{4}$ yd

C $24\frac{3}{4}$ yd

D $26\frac{3}{4}$ yd

E NH

22. Jeremy had 10.33 yards of flannel. He used 9.66 yd of flannel to make holiday decorations. How much flannel does he have left?

F 0.33 yd

G 0.50 yd

H 0.67 yd

J 1 yd

K NH

23. The directions said to travel $\frac{3}{10}$ mi from the highway to the town square, then travel $\frac{3}{5}$ mi on Route 15 to Tom's house. What is the total distance in miles from the highway to Tom's house?

A $\frac{9}{10}$ mi

B $\frac{4}{5}$ mi

C $\frac{7}{10}$ mi

D $\frac{1}{2}$ mi

E NH

24. A room measures $14\frac{1}{2}$ ft by 20 ft. Find the area of the room in square feet using the formula $A = l \times w$.

F 140 ft^2

G 200 ft^2

H 290 ft^2

J 330 ft^2

K NH

25. A tile setter is tiling a floor with tiles that measure $\frac{2}{3}$ ft on each side. If he uses 19 tiles along the wall, how long is the wall?

A $12\frac{1}{3}$ ft

B $12\frac{2}{3}$ ft

C $13\frac{1}{3}$ ft

D $13\frac{2}{3}$ ft

E NH

GO ON

Name_____ Class_____ Date_____

 SAT 10 Practice Test

26. Jei's cousin can walk about $\frac{3}{4}$ mile per hour.

At that rate, how many miles can she walk in 3 hours?

F $\frac{7}{8}$ mi

G $1\frac{1}{2}$ mi

H $2\frac{1}{4}$ mi

J $3\frac{1}{4}$ mi

K NH

27. Sarah picked a $5\frac{3}{4}$-pound pumpkin on Monday and a $3\frac{3}{8}$-pound pumpkin on Saturday.

$5\frac{3}{4}$ lb $3\frac{3}{8}$ lb

How many pounds did both pumpkins weigh all together?

A $5\frac{1}{2}$ lb

B $6\frac{1}{4}$ lb

C $8\frac{1}{8}$ lb

D $9\frac{1}{8}$ lb

E NH

28. Jason traveled 14.593 miles. Alyce traveled 29.193 miles. How many more miles did Alyce travel than Jason?

F 14.5

G 14.59

H 14.6

J 14.9

K NH

29. Myra bought these jeans for $10 off the price shown.

jeans
$40

What percent discount did she receive?

A 10%

B 20%

C 25%

D 30%

E NH

30. This oil drum was stored in Lila's garage.

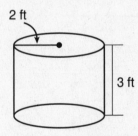

2 ft

3 ft

Lila calculated the volume of the oil drum to be about 37.68 ft³. If the drum is 90% full, what is the current capacity of the drum?

F 3.768 ft³

G 18.840 ft³

H 33.842 ft³

J 33.912 ft³

K NH

STOP

ITBS Practice Test

Read each question and choose the best answer. Then mark the space on the answer sheet for the answer you have chosen.

1. Anastasia was reviewing her company's travel mileage for the past four months. She recorded 42,381; 2580; 17,281; and 5326 miles. What was her company's total mileage for these months?

    A 67,568 mi

    B 67,668 mi

    C 66,568 mi

    D 67,567 mi

2. Miko had $2486 in her bank account last week. She then wanted to write a check for $3291. How much does she need to deposit before writing the check?

    F $805

    G $705

    H $820

    J $740

3. Marilyn got a loan to buy a new car. The monthly payment is $328.70. She has to make payments for five years. What is the total she will pay for the car?

    A $19,822

    B $19,722

    C over $20,000

    D less than $15,000

4. The navigation team for a planned spaceflight calculated that it will take 25 years to travel 4.2 light years. How many light years will the spacecraft cover each year?

    F 0.168 light year

    G 105 light years

    H 0.16 light year

    J 5.95 light years

5. Simplify $\frac{5}{12} + \frac{7}{20}$.

    A $\frac{12}{240}$

    B $\frac{48}{60}$

    C $\frac{23}{30}$

    D $\frac{23}{20}$

6. Simplify $\frac{13}{18} - \frac{7}{12}$.

    F 1

    G $\frac{6}{6}$

    H $\frac{5}{36}$

    J $\frac{6}{36}$

GO ON

ITBS Practice Test

7. Multiply $\frac{3}{8} \times \frac{1}{7}$.

  A $\frac{24}{56}$

  B $\frac{4}{15}$

  C $\frac{8}{21}$

  D $\frac{3}{56}$

8. What is the quotient when you divide $\frac{2}{3}$ by $\frac{5}{9}$?

  F $2\frac{7}{10}$

  G $\frac{10}{27}$

  H $1\frac{3}{5}$

  J $1\frac{1}{5}$

9. Find the sum: $2.013 + 28.7 + 7.21$.

  A 3.792

  B 30.3309

  C 12.093

  D 37.923

10. When you subtract 6.3 from 12.027, how many digits are there to the right of the decimal point in the answer?

  F 0

  G 1

  H 0

  J 3

11. Which statement is true of the following problem?

21.62×3.08

  A You must line up the decimal points before multiplying.

  B The answer has two digits to the right of the decimal point.

  C The answer is less than 67.

  D The answer is more than 68.

12. A rectangular field has an area of 26.04 km^2. Two sides are each 12 km long. What is the length of each of the other two sides?

  F 312. 48 km

  G 2.17 km

  H 12 km

  J 24 km

GO ON

ITBS Practice Test

13. Which of these is NOT true of the answer to the problem?

$$47.3193 \div 2.08$$

A It has more than four digits to the right of the decimal point.

B It can be written as a fraction.

C It is a rational number.

D It is an irrational number.

14. Maryann bought 8 CDs at $8.97 each. What did she pay for all eight?

F $112.12

G $71.76

H $8.97

J More than $72

15. In a relay race, the first runner ran 236 meters. The second runner ran 812 meters. The third runner ran 2007 meters. What was the total distance they ran?

A 1018 meters

B 3055 meters

C 30,550 meters

D 3000 meters

16. Samantha bought three magazines for $2.95 each, and two cards for $1.86 each. How much did she spend?

F $11.57

G $12.57

H $4.81

J $23.68

17. Evaluate the expression.

$$\frac{7}{12}\left(\frac{1}{3} + \frac{3}{4}\right) - \frac{5}{8}$$

A $\frac{1}{144}$

B $\frac{1}{12}$

C $\frac{1}{4}$

D $\frac{4}{144}$

18. Suppose you toss a coin and toss a single die. How many possible outcomes are there?

F 12

G 2

H 8

J 6

GO ON

ITBS Practice Test

19. Which algebraic expression describes the pattern 5, 7, 9, 11, 13, . . . ?

A $2x + 1$

B $2x + 3$

C add 10 each time

D add 2 to the tens digit each time

20. What is the missing value in the table below?

1	2	3	4
3	6	9	12
9	18	27	36
27	54	81	

F 72

G 108

H 27

J 48

21. What are the missing values in the table below?

n	2	4	6	8
$5n - 4$	6	16		

A 36 and 56

B 36 and 46

C 18 and 36

D 26 and 36

22. Jason's father drove 486 miles on vacation. The car used 33.3 gallons of fuel. Express the fuel consumption in miles per gallon, to the nearest tenth.

F 14.3 miles/gallon

G 13.6 miles/gallon

H 14.7 miles/gallon

J 14.6 miles/gallon

23. Which linear equation best fits the following data points?

(1, 3.1), (2, 4.8), (3, 6.7), (4, 9.2)

A $y = 2x + 2$

B $y = 3x - 5$

C $y = x + 4$

D $y = 2x + 1$

24. Which linear equation best fits the following data points?

(1, 1.2), (4, 9.8), (7, 18.6)

F $y = 3\frac{x}{3}$

G $y = 3x - 1$

H $y = 2x + 5$

J $y = 3x - 2$

GO ON

ITBS Practice Test

25. Which of these sets of numbers has elements that are all divisible by 3?

 A {12, 21, 27, 33}

 B {13, 23, 33, 43}

 C {21, 27, 19, 63}

 D {24, 9, 27, 83}

26. Which algebraic expression best describes the pattern?

3, 8, 13, 18, 23, 28, . . .

 F $5x - 2$

 G $3x + 7$

 H $10x + 3$

 J $x^2 - 7$

27. Which figure is NOT a quadrilateral?

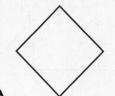

 A

 B

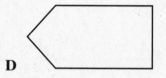

 C

 D

GO ON

ITBS Practice Test

28. Which of these is the area of the figure below?

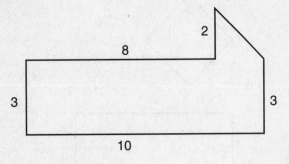

F 32 square units

G 52 square units

H 25 square units

J 30 square units

29. Which of these is the best estimate of the area of the figure below?

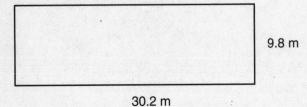

30.2 m

A 279 m²

B 300 m²

C 270 m²

D 310 m²

30. Of the numbers $\frac{4}{7}$, $\frac{7}{9}$, $\frac{8}{10}$, 0.71, and 0.59, which is the greatest?

F $\frac{7}{9}$

G $\frac{8}{10}$

H 0.71

J $\frac{4}{7}$

31. An employee of a large company was paid $48.75 for working 7.5 hours. What was the employee's rate of pay?

A $6.50/hour

B $6.25/hour

C $6.75/hour

D $7.50/hour

32. Larry recorded the number of hours he worked in each of the past five weeks; 32.6, 40.7, 37.4, 20.8, and 31.4. What is the mean number of hours per week worked over the five-week period?

F 32.6 hours

G 30.75 hours

H 32.58 hours

J 33 hours

ITBS Practice Test

33. Solve for x.

$$5x - 4 = 8 - x$$

A 0

B 1

C 3

D 2

34. Use rounding to estimate the difference, $13.98 - 7.36$.

F 8

G 5

H 6

J 7

35. Round 23.1743 to the hundredths place.

A 23.174

B 23.2

C 23.18

D 23.17

36. Which of the following would you estimate to be $1\frac{1}{2}$?

F $\frac{4}{7} + \frac{8}{9}$

G $\frac{6}{7} + \frac{4}{5}$

H $\frac{8}{9} + \frac{11}{12}$

J $\frac{1}{7} + \frac{5}{7}$

37. Which of the following would you estimate to be 0?

A $\frac{4}{7} - \frac{5}{8}$

B $\frac{8}{9} - \frac{1}{3}$

C $\frac{12}{11} - \frac{1}{4}$

D $\frac{5}{6} - \frac{1}{8}$

GO ON

38. Which is the best estimate for the length of the side labeled *x*?

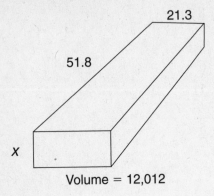

21.3

51.8

x

Volume = 12,012

F 8
G 12
H 13
J 16

39. Which of these is an underestimate of the sum of 21.4, 30.8, 7.4, and 16.3?

A 77
B 78
C 76
D 74

40. Which of these is the best estimate of the sum?

83.4
16.8
7.3
+ 12.4

F 108
G 119
H 130
J 1,199

STOP

Name _____ Class _____ Date _____

TerraNova Practice Test

Part 1

Read each question and choose the best answer. Then mark the space on the answer sheet for the answer you have chosen.

1 $\frac{3}{8} + \frac{1}{6} =$

    A $\frac{27}{48}$

    B $\frac{13}{24}$

    C $\frac{2}{7}$

    D $\frac{1}{6}$

    E None of these

2 $\frac{1}{2} \times \frac{2}{3} =$

    F $\frac{1}{3}$

    G $\frac{2}{5}$

    H $\frac{1}{6}$

    J $\frac{1}{2}$

3 $-96 + (-12) =$

    A -84

    B   84

    C -108

    D   108

    E None of these

4 $0.4\overline{)10.16}$

    F   0.0254

    G   0.254

    H   2.54

    J   25.4

    K None of these

5 **85% of 32 =**

    A   272

    B   37.6

    C   27.2

    D   0.272

    E None of these

6 **8 ÷ 11 =**

    F   0.72

    G   0.727

    H $0.7\overline{2}$

    J $0.\overline{727}$

    K None of these

7 **2(10 − 8) + 8 ÷ 4 =**

    A 14

    B 6

    C 5

    D 3

    E None of these

>**GO ON**

TerraNova Practice Test

8 Which is the name of this polyhedron?

F   Triangular pyramid

G   Rectangular pyramid

H   Hexagonal pyramid

J   Octagonal pyramid

9 A fish tank is a rectangular prism with dimensions 30 inches by 20 inches by 16 inches. What is the maximum volume of water it can hold?

A   480 in^3

B   960 in^3

C   4,800 in^3

D   9,600 in^3

10 Which addition problem does the model represent?

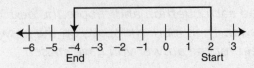

F $2 + (-4) = -2$

G $-4 + (-6) = -10$

H $-4 + (-4) = -8$

J $2 + (-6) = -4$

11 What number can go in the box to make the sentence true?

$(\square - 6) \div 5 = 30$

A   150

B   156

C   144

D   12

12 Which fraction forms a terminating decimal?

F $\dfrac{6}{11}$

G $\dfrac{4}{9}$

H $\dfrac{3}{5}$

J $\dfrac{5}{12}$

GO ON

TerraNova Practice Test

13 Find the ratio of the number of shaded squares to the total number of squares.

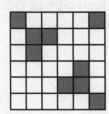

A $\frac{1}{4}$

B $\frac{1}{3}$

C $\frac{3}{1}$

D $\frac{4}{1}$

14 A 10-foot ladder leans against a building with the base of the ladder 6 feet from the building. How high is the point where the ladder touches the building?

F 9 ft

G 8 ft

H 7 ft

J 6 ft

15 Which fraction, percent, or decimal does the shaded area represent?

A 24%

B $\frac{24}{10}$

C 2.4

D $\frac{24}{100}$%

16 Ken and Lu decide to keep a bar graph showing how many books each of them read for four months. In which month was the total books read the greatest?

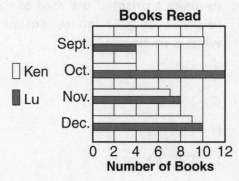

F September

G October

H November

J December

17 Tsao Lin is evaluating shoe box racks for use in a shoe manufacturing plant. The number of boxes in the rack must be divisible by both 6 and 8. Which of the following rack capacities can she use?

A 112

B 184

C 192

D 204

TerraNova Practice Test

Part 2

18 An artist pours 1,701 cubic centimeters of plaster into a mold to make a prism. If the area of the prism's base is 81 square centimeters, what is its height?

F   21 cm

G   30 cm

H   1,541 cm

J   137,781 cm

19 How do you find the volume of a cylinder?

A   Multiply the base circumference times the height.

B   Multiply $\frac{1}{2}$ the base circumference times the height.

C   Multiply the base area times the height.

D   Multiply $\frac{1}{2}$ the base area times the height.

20 Use the formula $c = \frac{f}{8}$ to change fluid ounces (f) into cups (c). How many cups are equal to 48 fluid ounces?

F   4 cups

G   6 cups

H   8 cups

J   10 cups

21 *QRST ~ JKLM.* Which side in *QRST* corresponds to $\overline{JK}$?

A $\overline{QT}$

B $\overline{QR}$

C $\overline{RS}$

D $\overline{TS}$

22 △*ABC ~* △*DEF.* Find *x.*

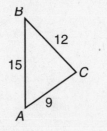

F $x = 6$

G $x = 5$

H $x = 4$

J $x = 3$

23 A statue is 12 feet high. Find the largest scale you can use for a model statue if it must fit into a 3-inch-high box.

A   1 in.:4 ft

B   1 in.:3 ft

C   3 in.:1 ft

D   4 in.:1 ft

TerraNova Practice Test

24 Which expression would give you the best estimate of 49% of 377?

F 49% of 300

G 49% of 350

H 50% of 350

J 50% of 380

25 Mike mows lawns. He charges $3.50 per lawn. Mike earned $21.00 this week. How many lawns did he mow?

A 8

B 7

C 6

D 5

26 Melora volunteers at the library every 14th day and at the hospital every 12th day. On which day will she volunteer at both the library and the hospital?

F Day 96

G Day 72

H Day 84

J Day 108

27 As shown in the table, the cost of renting a video camera depends on the number of days you rent it. Which equation represents the relationship between cost and number of days?

Days	2	4	5	7
Cost ($)	12	24	30	42

A $C = 3d$

B $C = 5d$

C $C = 6d$

D $C = 12d$

28 Which number would be the 12th term in the sequence described by this table?

n	1	2	3	4
$\frac{n}{3}$	$\frac{1}{3}$	$\frac{2}{3}$	1	$1\frac{1}{3}$

F 12

G 4

H $\frac{1}{12}$

J $\frac{3}{12}$

29 Find the area of the figure.

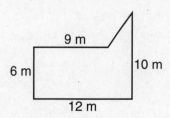

A 24 m^2

B 36 m^2

C 42 m^2

D 78 m^2

GO ON

TerraNova Practice Test

30 Find an expression describing the rule for the sequence in the table.

Term Number (n)	1	2	3	4	5
Number in Sequence	9	10	11	12	13

F $n + 9$

G $9n$

H $8n$

J $n + 8$

31 Stan makes pins from shells and sells them for 75¢ each. How many pins would he need to sell to earn $12?

A 10 pins

B 12 pins

C 14 pins

D 16 pins

32 In a proportion, which ratio could be shown equal to $\frac{6}{7}$?

F $\frac{24}{25}$

G $\frac{18}{21}$

H $\frac{13}{14}$

J $\frac{12}{18}$

33 Jan runs at a rate of 6 miles per hour. If m = the number of miles Jan runs and h = the number of hours, find an equation to represent the number of miles she runs in h hours.

A $m = \frac{h}{6}$

B $h = 6m$

C $m = 6h$

D $h = m + 6$

34 Alex uses the formula $q = \frac{c}{4}$ to change cups (c) into quarts (q). He has 16 cups of fresh-squeezed juice. How many quarts of fresh-squeezed juice does he have?

F 4 qt

G 8 qt

H 12 qt

J 64 qt

35 Solve for x.

$$-3x + 5 = -1$$

A $-1\frac{1}{3}$

B -2

C 2

D -6

GO ON

TerraNova Practice Test

36 The table below represents the equation $y = -4x + 8$. Use the table to solve the related equation $0 = -4x + 8$.

x	−2	−1	0	1	2
y	16	12	8	4	0

F $x = 0$

G $x = -2$

H $x = -8$

J $x = 2$

37 Which shows the graph of the inequality $x \geq -7$?

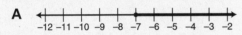

A

B

C

D

38 The value of Myra's stamp collection has gone up 20% since last year. If it was worth $450 last year, how much is it worth now?

F $430

G $470

H $540

J $9,000

39 Which is 4,250,000,000 written in scientific notation?

A 0.425×10^{10}

B 4.25×10^{8}

C 4.25×10^{9}

D 425×10^{7}

40 Find the rule for the translation of *ABCD*.

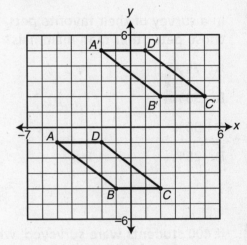

F $(x, y) \rightarrow (x + 3, y + 6)$

G $(x, y) \rightarrow (x - 3, y - 6)$

H $(x, y) \rightarrow (x + 5, y + 8)$

J $(x, y) \rightarrow (x - 5, y - 8)$

> GO ON

TerraNova Practice Test

Use this graph for Items 41–43.

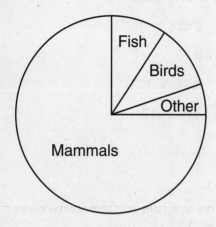

41 In a survey of their favorite pets, about what percent of students chose pets other than mammals?

A 75%

B 50%

C 30%

D 25%

42 If 400 students were surveyed, which is the best estimate for the number choosing mammals?

F 100

G 300

H 200

J 150

43 About what percent of the students surveyed chose fish?

A 90%

B 30%

C 25%

D 10%

GO ON

TerraNova Practice Test

44 This stem-and-leaf diagram shows test scores for Mr. Ramirez's class. What is the class's median test score?

Stem	Leaf
7	4 5 5 6 8
8	0 1 4 4 7
9	3 4 6

F 87

G 84

H 81

J 80

45 The table shows the results for several rolls of two number cubes. Use the table to find the experimental probability of rolling a sum of 5.

Rolls (Sum)	2	3	4	5	6	7	8	9	10	11	12
Frequency	1	4	5	7	10	12	6	3	5	1	2

A $\frac{1}{6}$

B $\frac{1}{8}$

C $\frac{1}{9}$

D $\frac{1}{10}$

46 Angela spins a spinner with the numbers 1–6 on it. What is the probability that she will spin a 2 three times in a row?

F $\frac{1}{216}$

G $\frac{1}{52}$

H $\frac{1}{36}$

J $\frac{1}{18}$

GO ON

TerraNova Practice Test

47 Which is the mean for this data set?

5, 2, 4, 40, 11, 5, 9, 6, 8

A 5.5

B 5

C 9

D 10

48 The results of a survey showed that 88% of the people would vote in favor of the town referendum to improve road conditions. Suppose 940 people vote. About how many people can you expect to vote in favor of the referendum?

F about 500

G about 827

H about 880

J about 450

49 Without looking, June picked a marble out of a bag containing 4 red, 6 blue, and 8 yellow marbles. Find the probability that the marble she picked was blue.

A $\frac{1}{6}$

B $\frac{1}{5}$

C $\frac{1}{3}$

D $\frac{1}{2}$

50 An angle measures 135°. Which of the following describes or gives the measure of a complement and a supplement of the angle?

F 45°; 45°

G no complement; 55°

H 35°; 55°

J no complement; 45°

51 $\triangle D'E'F'$ is the reflection of $\triangle DEF$ across the *x*-axis. Find the coordinates of the vertices of $\triangle D'E'F'$.

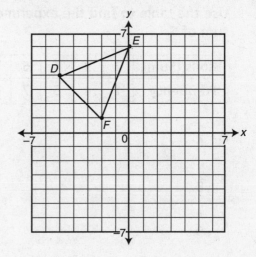

A $D'(-5, -4)$, $E'(0, -6)$ $F'(-2, -1)$

B $D'(5, -4)$, $E'(0, 6)$ $F'(2, 1)$

C $D'(5, -4)$, $E'(0, -6)$ $F'(2, -1)$

D $D'(-5, 4)$, $E'(0, 6)$ $F'(-2, 1)$

> GO ON

TerraNova Practice Test

52 Which is the perimeter of the garden?

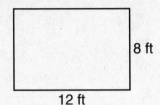

8 ft

12 ft

F   48 ft

G   20 ft

H   96 ft

J   40 ft

53 Karen needs to paint the outside of the storehouse shown. She will not paint the roof. A gallon of paint covers about 400 square feet. How many gallons will she need to buy?

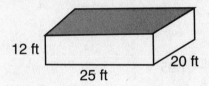

12 ft

20 ft

25 ft

A   2 gal

B   3 gal

C   4 gal

D   5 gal

54 Classify the triangle by its sides and by its angles.

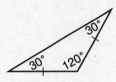

30°   30°   120°

F   acute scalene

G   obtuse scalene

H   acute isosceles

J   obtuse isosceles

55 Which of these rectangles is similar to a rectangle that measures 15 cm by 18 cm?

A   3 cm by 6 cm

B   5 cm by 9 cm

C   10 cm by 12 cm

D   12 cm by 14 cm

56 Use the figure to find a pair of perpendicular lines.

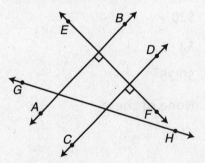

F $\overleftrightarrow{AB}$ and $\overleftrightarrow{CD}$

G $\overleftrightarrow{AB}$ and $\overleftrightarrow{GH}$

H $\overleftrightarrow{CD}$ and $\overleftrightarrow{EF}$

J $\overleftrightarrow{CD}$ and $\overleftrightarrow{GH}$

TerraNova Practice Test

Part 3

1 $38.06 + 7.3 =$

A 38.79

B 45.39

C 45.9

D 44.36

E None of these

2 $38 - (-15) =$

F 23

G 33

H 43

J 53

K None of these

3 5% of $50 =

A $25

B $20

C $2

D $0.25

E None of these

4 $5.6 \times 0.14 =$

F 7.84

G 7.64

H 0.784

J 0.0764

K None of these

5 $65 - 20 \div (2 + 3) =$

A 9

B 15

C 61

D 69

E None of these

6 $6 - 1.05 =$

F 5.94

G 5.05

H 5.04

J 4.95

E None of these

GO ON

TerraNova Practice Test

7 $10\frac{1}{5} - 8\frac{4}{5} =$

A $1\frac{2}{5}$

B $2\frac{3}{5}$

C $2\frac{2}{5}$

D $1\frac{3}{5}$

E None of these

8 $5\frac{3}{4} \div 1\frac{1}{3} =$

F $7\frac{2}{3}$

G $5\frac{1}{4}$

H $4\frac{5}{16}$

J $3\frac{2}{3}$

K None of these

9 $\frac{5}{21} + \frac{4}{7} =$

A $\frac{9}{28}$

B $\frac{9}{21}$

C $\frac{17}{21}$

D $\frac{6}{7}$

E None of these

10 $30 \div 0.0005 =$

F 6

G 600

H 6,000

J 60,000

K None of these

11 $\frac{21}{48} \times \frac{8}{45} =$

A $\frac{1}{10}$

B $\frac{7}{90}$

C $\frac{1}{15}$

D $\frac{7}{8}$

E None of these

12 $-50 \times 7 =$

F -35

G 300

H 350

J -350

K None of these

GO ON

TerraNova Practice Test

13 $15 + 3(2 - 1) - 6 \div 2 =$

    A 17

    B 15

    C 7

    D 6

    E None of these

14 $-56 \div (-8) =$

    F -448

    G 7

    H -7

    J 448

    K None of these

15 $\dfrac{16 - 4}{3} \times 7 - 8 =$

    A 12

    B 13

    C 20

    D 28

    E None of these

16 $26 + (-18) =$

    F -44

    G 8

    H -8

    J 44

    K None of these

17 15 is 30% of what number?

    A 5

    B 45

    C 90

    D 100

    E None of these

18 15% of 40 =

    F $2\dfrac{2}{3}$

    G $\dfrac{5}{9}$

    H 6

    J 60

    K None of these

19 $48 - 36 \div (4 + 2) =$

    A 42

    B 41

    C 2

    D 5

    E None of these

20 6 is what percent of 24?

    F 20%

    G 25%

    H 30%

    J 40%

    K None of these

Name _____ Class _____ Date _____

Screening Test Report

Mathematics Concepts	Test Items	Proficient? Yes or No
Number Properties and Operations		
Identify the place value and actual value of digits in whole numbers.	1	
Connect model, word, or number using various models and representations for whole numbers, fractions, and decimals.	2	
Order or compare whole numbers, decimals, or fractions.	3	
Use benchmarks (well known numbers used as meaningful points for comparison) for whole numbers, decimals, or fractions in contexts (e.g., $\frac{1}{2}$ and .5 may be used as benchmarks for fractions and decimals between 0 and 1.00).	4	
Add and subtract whole numbers.	5, 6	
Add and subtract fractions with like denominators.	7, 8	
Add and subtract decimals through hundredths.	9, 10	
Multiply and divide whole numbers up to three-digit by two-digit.	11, 12	
Solve application problems involving whole number operations.	13	
Use simple ratios to describe problem situations.	14	
Identify odd and even numbers.	15	
Identify factors of whole numbers.	16	
Apply basic properties of operations.	17	
Measurement		
Identify the attribute that is appropriate to measure in a given situation.	18	
Select or use appropriate measurement instruments such as ruler, meter stick, clock, thermometer, or other scaled instruments.	19	
Solve problems involving perimeter of plane figures, providing the formula as part of the problem.	20	
Solve problems involving area of rectangles, providing the formula as part of the problem.	21	
Select or use appropriate type of unit for the attribute being measured such as length, time, or temperature.	22	
Geometry		
Describe (informally) real world objects using simple plane figures (e.g., triangles, rectangles, squares and circles) and simple solid figures (e.g., cubes, spheres, and cylinders).	23	
Identify or draw angles and other geometric figures in the plane.	24	
Describe attributes of two- and three-dimensional shapes.	25	

Mathematics Concepts	Test Items	Proficient? Yes or No
Geometry *(continued)*		
Assemble simple plane shapes to construct a given shape.	26	
Recognize two-dimensional faces of three-dimensional shapes.	27	
Data Analysis and Probability		
Interpret pictograms, bar graphs, circle graphs, line graphs, line plots, tables, and tallies.	28	
Read or interpret a single set of data.	29	
List all possible outcomes of a given situation or event.	30	
Represent the probability of a given outcome.	31	
Algebra		
Recognize, describe, or extend numerical patterns.	32	
Find the value of the unknown in a whole number sentence.	33	
Express simple mathematical relationships using number sentences.	34, 36	
Graph or interpret points with whole number or letter coordinates on grids or in the first quadrant of the coordinate plane.	35	

Student Comments: _____

_____

_____

_____

_____

Parent Comments: _____

_____

_____

_____

_____

Teacher Comments: _____

_____

_____

_____

_____

Name _____ Class _____ Date _____

Benchmark Test 1 Report

Mathematics Concepts	NAEP Objective(s)	Test Items	Number Correct	Proficient? Yes or No	Skills Review and Practice
Decimals and Integers					
Make estimates appropriate to a given situation by identifying when estimation is appropriate and selecting the appropriate method of estimation.	N2b, N2d	1, 2, 3	□/3		103
Solve problems involving conversions within the metric system.	M2b, M2c	4, 5, 6	□/3		106
Order or compare integers using various representations.	N1i	7, 8, 9	□/3		108
Calculate, use, and interpret the mean, median, mode, or range of a set of data.	D2a, b, c	10, 11, 12, 13, 14, 15	□/6		112
Exponents, Factors, and Fractions					
Write and evaluate algebraic expressions involving exponents and the order of operations.	A3b	16, 17, 18	□/3		123
Express or interpret numbers using scientific notation from real-world contexts.	N1f	19, 20, 21	□/3		124
Use divisibility or remainders in problem situations.	N5d	22, 23, 24	□/3		125
Recognize prime numbers and find the prime factorization of integers.	N5b	25, 26, 27	□/3		126
Solve problems involving positive and negative fractions.	N3a, g	28, 29, 30	□/3		127
Compare and order fractions.	N1j, N3g	31, 32, 33	□/3		128
Order or compare fractions and decimals using various representations.	N1j, N3g	34, 35, 36	□/3		130, 131, 132

*NAEP (National Assessment of Educational Progress Mathematics Objectives)

N = Number Properties and Operations; M = Measurement; G = Geometry; D = Data Analysis and Probability; A = Algebra

Student Comments: _____

_____

_____

_____

_____

_____

_____

_____

_____

_____

Parent Comments: _____

_____

_____

_____

_____

_____

_____

_____

_____

_____

_____

_____

Teacher Comments: _____

_____

_____

_____

_____

_____

_____

_____

_____

_____

_____

_____

Benchmark Test 2 Report

Mathematics Concepts	NAEP Objective(s)	Test Items	Number Correct	Proficient? Yes or No	Skills Review and Practice
Operations with Fractions					
Perform addition and subtraction computations with fractions and mixed numbers.	N3a, g	1, 2, 3	□/3		133, 134, 135
Perform multiplication computations with fractions and mixed numbers.	N3a, g	4, 5, 6	□/3		136
Perform division computations with fractions and mixed numbers.	N3a, g	7, 8, 9	□/3		137
Solve problems involving conversions within the customary measurement system.	M2b, N3g	10, 11, 12	□/3		140, 141
Equations and Inequalities					
Write and evaluate algebraic expressions.	A3a	13, 14, 15	□/3		113
Solve one-step linear equations.	A4a	16, 17, 18	□/3		116
Analyze situations using two-step equations.	A4a	19, 20, 21	□/3		117
Solve two-step linear equations.	A4a	22, 23, 24	□/3		118
Analyze situations and solve mathematical or real-world problems using two-step equations.	A4a, c	25, 26, 27	□/3		119
Analyze situations and solve mathematical or real-world problems using linear inequalities symbolically or graphically.	A4c	28, 29, 30	□/3		120
Solve one-step linear inequalities.	A4a	31, 32, 33	□/3		121, 122

*NAEP (National Assessment of Educational Progress Mathematics Objectives)

N = Number Properties and Operations; M = Measurement; G = Geometry; D = Data Analysis and Probability; A = Algebra

Student Comments:_____

_____

_____

_____

_____

_____

_____

_____

_____

_____

Parent Comments:_____

_____

_____

_____

_____

_____

_____

_____

_____

_____

_____

Teacher Comments:_____

_____

_____

_____

_____

_____

_____

_____

_____

_____

_____

_____

Benchmark Test 3 Report

Mathematics Concepts	NAEP Objective(s)	Test Items	Number Correct	Proficient? Yes or No	Skills Review and Practice
Ratios, Rates, and Proportions					
Use fractions to represent and express ratios.	N4a, b	1, 2, 3	☐/3		142
Use proportional reasoning to solve problems involving unit rates.	N4b, c	4, 5, 6	☐/3		143
Use fractions to represent and express proportions and solve proportions using appropriate strategies.	N4b, c	7, 8, 9	☐/3		145, 146
Use appropriate strategies to solve proportions involving similar figures.	N4c, M1k	10, 11, 12	☐/3		147
Use proportional reasoning in solving problems involving scale drawings.	N4c, M1k	13, 14, 15	☐/3		148
Percents					
Solve problems involving percentages.	N1i, N4d	16, 17, 18	☐/3		149, 151, 152
Order or compare rational numbers, including percents, using various representations.	N1i, N4d	19, 20, 21	☐/3		150, 151
Solve problems involving percents using various strategies and representations.	N1i, N4d	22, 23, 24	☐/3		150, 152
Identify and represent proportional relationships in meaningful contexts.	N4d, A2g	25, 26, 27	☐/3		153, 154
Solve problems involving percentages, including part/whole relationships.	N4d	28, 29, 30	☐/3		150, 155
Solve problems involving percentages, including tax, discount, tips, and markup.	N4d	31, 32, 33	☐/3		155
Solve problems involving percents and percent applications.	N4d	34, 35, 36	☐/3		156

Student Comments: _____

_____

_____

_____

_____

_____

_____

_____

_____

_____

Parent Comments: _____

_____

_____

_____

_____

_____

_____

_____

_____

_____

_____

Teacher Comments: _____

_____

_____

_____

_____

_____

_____

_____

_____

_____

Benchmark Test 4 Report

Mathematics Concepts	NAEP Objective(s)	Test Items	Number Correct	Proficient? Yes or No	Skills Review and Practice
Geometry					
Describe and identify the measurement and properties of supplementary and complementary angles.	G1c	1, 2, 3	☐/3		158, 159
Classify the types and properties of triangles.	G1f, G3f	4, 5, 6	☐/3		161
Classify the types and properties of quadrilaterals.	G1c, f, G3f	7, 8, 9	☐/3		162
Investigate congruent figures and apply congruency relationships to find missing measurements.	G2e	10, 11, 12	☐/3		164
Create, use, and interpret circle graphs for data analysis.	D1b	13, 14, 15	☐/3		165, 166
Geometry and Measurement					
Estimate the size of an object with respect to the given measurements of length and area.	M1c	16, 17, 18	☐/3		167
Solve mathematical or real-world problems involving the areas of parallelograms and triangles.	M1h	19, 20, 21	☐/3		168, 169
Solve mathematical or real-world problems involving the circumferences and areas of circles.	M1h	22, 23, 24	☐/3		170
Establish and apply benchmarks for rational numbers and common irrational numbers.	N2a	25, 26, 27	☐/3		171
Use the Pythagorean Theorem to solve problems.	G3d	28, 29, 30	☐/3		172
Use spatial reasoning to identify, define, or describe geometric shapes in three-dimensional space.	G1c, f	31, 32, 33	☐/3		173

Benchmark Test 4 Report

Mathematics Concepts	NAEP Objective(s)	Test Items	Number Correct	Proficient? Yes or No	Skills Review and Practice
Geometry and Measurement *(continued)*					
Solve mathematical or real-world problems involving the volumes of rectangular prisms and cylinders.	M1j	34, 35, 36	☐ / 3		175

*NAEP (National Assessment of Educational Progress Mathematics Objectives)

N = Number Properties and Operations; M = Measurement; G = Geometry; D = Data Analysis and Probability; A = Algebra

Student Comments: _____

_____

_____

_____

_____

_____

_____

Parent Comments: _____

_____

_____

_____

_____

_____

_____

Teacher Comments: _____

_____

_____

_____

_____

_____

_____

Name _____ Class _____ Date _____

Benchmark Test 5 Report

Mathematics Concepts	NAEP Objective(s)	Test Items	Number Correct	Proficient? Yes or No	Skills Review and Practice
Patterns and Rules					
Generalize a pattern appearing in a numerical sequence or table using words or symbols.	A1a, b	1, 2, 3	⬜ /3		178
Recognize, describe, or extend patterns using tables, graphs, words, or symbols.	A1a, b	4, 5, 6	⬜ /3		177, 179
Write, analyze, and interpret function rules.	A2b, A3a	7, 8, 9	⬜ /3		180, 181
Analyze or interpret linear relationships expressed in graphs.	A2b	10, 11, 12	⬜ /3		181, 182
Solve problems involving percentages, including compounding interest.	N4d, A2g	13, 14, 15	⬜ /3		183
Use, evaluate, and transform common formulas.	A4e	16, 17, 18	⬜ /3		185
Graphing in the Coordinate Plane					
Use ordered pairs to graph and interpret points on a coordinate plane.	A2c	19, 20, 21	⬜ /3		186
Analyze situations and solve problems using linear equations symbolically or graphically.	A2c, A4c	22, 23, 24, 25, 26, 27	⬜ /6		187
Interpret relationships between linear expressions and graphs of lines by identifying and computing slope.	A4d	28, 29, 30	⬜ /3		188
Identify functions as linear or non-linear.	A1e	31, 32, 33	⬜ /3		189
Recognize or describe the effect of a translation on two-dimensional geometric shapes.	G2c	34, 35, 36	⬜ /3		191
Identify lines of symmetry in plane figures and describe the effect of reflections on two-dimensional geometric shapes.	G2a, c	37, 38, 39	⬜ /3		192

Student Comments: _____

_____

_____

_____

_____

_____

_____

_____

_____

_____

_____

Parent Comments: _____

_____

_____

_____

_____

_____

_____

_____

_____

_____

_____

Teacher Comments: _____

_____

_____

_____

_____

_____

_____

_____

_____

_____

_____

NAEP Mathematics Assessment Framework

NUMBER PROPERTIES AND OPERATIONS	TEST ITEMS
1) Number sense	
a) Use place value to model and describe integers and decimals.	
b) Model or describe rational numbers or numerical relationships using number lines and diagrams.	69
d) Write or rename rational functions.	20
e) Recognize, translate between, or apply multiple representations of rational numbers in meaningful contexts.	
f) Express or interpret numbers using scientific notation from real life contexts.	17
g) Find or model absolute value or apply to problem situations.	
i) Order or compare rational numbers using various models and representations.	4
j) Order or compare rational numbers including very large and small integers, and decimals and fractions close to zero.	
2) Estimation	
a) Establish or apply benchmarks for rational numbers and common irrational numbers in contexts.	
b) Make estimates appropriate to a given situation by: identifying when estimation is appropriate, determinating the level of accuracy needed, selecting the appropriate method of estimation, or analyzing the effect of an estimation method on the accuracy of results.	1
c) Verify solutions or determine the reasonableness of results in a variety of situations including calculator and computer results.	
d) Estimate square or cube roots of numbers less than 1,000 between two whole numbers.	2
3) Number operations	
a) Perform computations with rational numbers.	23, 24, 26
d) Describe the effect of multiplying and dividing by numbers.	
e) Provide a mathematical argument to explain operations with two or more fractions.	
f) Interpret rational number operations and the relationship between them.	
g) Solve application problems involving rational numbers and operations using exact answers or estimates as appropriate.	21, 22
4) Ratios and proportional reasoning	
a) Use ratios to describe problem situations.	27
b) Use fractions to represent and express ratios and proportions.	29, 30
c) Use proportional reasoning to model and solve problems.	28, 32, 33
d) Solve problems involving percentages.	34, 35, 36, 37
5) Properties of number and operations	
a) Describe odd and even integers and how they behave under different operations.	
b) Recognize, find, or use factors, multiples, or prime factorization.	19, 67
c) Recognize or use prime and composite numbers to solve problems.	
d) Use divisibility or remainders in problem settings.	18
e) Apply basic properties of operations.	
f) Explain or justify a mathematical concept or relationship.	

MEASUREMENT	TEST ITEMS
1) Measuring physical attributes	
b) Compare objects with respect to length, area, volume, angle measurement, weight, or mass.	48
c) Estimate the size of an object with respect to a given measurement attribute.	
g) Select or use appropriate measurement instrument to determine or create a given length, area, volume, angle, weight, or mass.	25
h) Solve mathematical or real-world problems involving perimeter or area of plane figures such as triangles, rectangles, circles, or composite figures.	49, 50, 51
j) Solve problems involving volume or surface area of rectangular solids, cylinders, prisms, or composite shapes.	53, 66
k) Solve problems involving indirect measurement such as finding the height of a building by comparing its shadow with the height and shadow of a known object.	31
l) Solve problems involving rates such as speed or population density.	
2) Systems of measurement	
a) Select or use appropriate type of unit for the attribute being measured such as length, area, angle, time, or volume.	
b) Solve problems involving conversions within the same measurement system such as conversions involving square inches and square feet.	
c) Estimate the measure of an object in one system given the measure of that object in another system and the approximate conversion factor.	3
d) Determine appropriate size of unit of measurement in problem situation involving such attributes as length, area, or volume.	
e) Determine appropriate accuracy of measurement in problem situations and find the measure to that degree of accuracy.	
f) Construct or solve problems involving scale drawings.	
GEOMETRY	TEST ITEMS
1) Dimension and shape	
a) Draw or describe a path of shortest length between points to solve problems in context.	
b) Identify a geometric object given written description of its properties.	42, 46
c) Identify, define, or describe geometric shapes in the plane and in 3-dimensional space given a visual representation.	39, 41
d) Draw or sketch from a written description polygons, circles, or semicircles.	
e) Represent or describe a three-dimensional situation in a two-dimensional drawing using perspective.	
f) Demonstrate an understanding about the two- and three-dimensional shapes in our world through identifying, drawing, modeling, building, or taking apart.	43
2) Transformation of shapes and preservation of properties	
a) Identify lines of symmetry in plane figures or recognize and classify types of symmetries of plane figures.	
c) Recognize or informally describe the effect of a transformation on two-dimensional geometric shapes.	

GEOMETRY continued	TEST ITEMS
d) Predict results of combining, subdividing, and changing shapes of place figures and solids	
e) Justify relationships of congruence and similarity, and apply these relationships using scaling and proportional reasoning.	
f) For similar figures, identify and use the relationships of conservation of angle and of proportionality of side length and perimeter.	45
3) Relationships between geometric figures	
b) Apply geometric properties and relationships in solving simple problems in two- and three-dimensions.	28, 40, 48
c) Represent problem situations with simple geometric models to solve mathematical or real-world problems.	
d) Use the Pythagorean theorem to solve problems.	52, 70
f) Describe or analyze simple properties of, or relationships between, triangles, quadrilaterals, and other polygonal plane figures.	44
g) Describe or analyze properties and relationships of parallel or intersecting lines.	
4) Position and direction	
a) Describe relative positions of points and lines using the geometric ideas of midpoint, points on common line through a common point, parallelism, or perpendicularity.	
b) Describe the intersection of two or more geometric figures in the plane.	
c) Visualize or describe the cross-section of a solid.	
d) Represent geometric figures using rectangular coordinates on a plane.	
5) Mathematical reasoning	
a) Make and test a geometric conjecture about regular polygons.	
DATA ANALYSIS AND PROBABILITY	TEST ITEMS
1) Data representation	
a) Read or interpret data, including interpolating or extrapolating from data.	47, 68
b) Given a set of data, complete a graph and then solve a problem using the data in the graph (circle graphs, histograms, bar graphs, line graphs, scatterplots).	
c) Solve problems by estimating and computing with data from a single set or across sets of data.	
d) Given a graph or a set of data, determine whether information is represented effectively and appropriately (circle graphs, histograms, bar graphs, line graphs, scatterplots).	
e) Compare and contrast the effectiveness of different representations of the same data.	
2) Characteristics of data sets	
a) Calculate, use, or interpret mean, median, mode, or range.	5
b) Describe how mean, median, mode, range, or interquartile ranges relate to the shape of distribution.	6
c) Identify outliers and determine their effect on mean, median, mode, or range.	
d) Using appropriate statistical measures, compare two or more data sets describing the same characteristic for two different populations or subsets of the same population.	

DATA ANALYSIS AND PROBABILITY continued	TEST ITEMS
e) Visually choose the line that best fits given a scatterplot and informally explain the meaning of the line. Use the line to make predictions.	
3) Experiments and samples	
a) Given a sample, identify possible sources of bias in sampling.	
b) Distinguish between a random and non-random sample.	61
d) Evaluate the design of an experiment.	
4) Probability	
a) Analyze a situation that involves probability of an independent event.	
b) Determine the theoretical probability of simple and compound events in familiar contexts.	62
c) Estimate the probability of simple and compound events through experimentation or simulation.	
d) Distinguish between experimental and theoretical probability.	63
e) Determine the sample space for a given situation.	
f) Use a sample space to determine the probability of the possible outcomes of an event.	
g) Represent probability using fractions, decimals, and percents.	
h) Determine the probability of independent and dependent events.	
j) Interpret probabilities within a given context.	

ALGEBRA	TEST ITEMS
1) Patterns, relations, and functions	
a) Recognize, describe, or extend numerical and geometric patterns using tables, graphs, words, or symbols.	54, 60
b) Generalize a pattern appearing in a numerical sequence or table or graph using words or symbols.	55
c) Analyze or create patterns, sequences, or linear functions given a rule.	64
e) Identify functions as linear or non-linear or contrast distinguishing properties of function from tables, graphs, or equations.	59
f) Interpret the meaning of slope or intercepts in linear functions.	58, 68
2) Algebraic representations	
a) Translate between different representations of linear expressions using symbols, graphs, tables, diagrams, or written descriptions.	56
b) Analyze or interpret linear relationships expressed in symbols, graphs, tables, diagrams, or written descriptions.	
c) Graph or interpret points that are represented by ordered pairs of numbers on a rectangular coordinate system.	
d) Solve problems involving coordinate pairs on the rectangular coordinate system.	57
e) Make, validate, and justify conclusions and generalizations about linear relationships.	
g) Identify or represent functional relationships in meaningful contexts including proportional, linear, and common non-linear in tables, graphs, words, or symbols.	

ALGEBRA continued	TEST ITEMS
3) Variables, expressions, and operations	
a) Write algebraic expressions, equations, or inequalities to represent the situation.	7, 9, 14
b) Perform basic operations, using appropriate tools, on linear algebraic expressions.	8
4) Equations and inequalities	
a) Solve linear equations or inequalities.	12, 15, 16
b) Interpret "=" as an equivalence between two expressions and use this interpretation to solve problems.	
c) Analyze situations or solve problems using linear equations and inequalities with rational coefficients symbolically or graphically.	10, 11, 13
d) Interpret relationships between symbolic linear expressions and graphs of lines by identifying and computing slope and intercepts.	
e) Use and evaluate common formulas.	

Correlation Chart: Practice Test to the SAT 10 Standards for Grade 7

SAT 10 Standards for Grade 7	Process Clusters	Test Items
MATHEMATICS: PROBLEM SOLVING		
Number Sense and Operations		
Identify the place value of a digit in a whole or decimal number	Communication and Representation	9
Identify alternative representations of rational numbers		4, 5, 6, 10
Identify and use order of operation rules		14
Translate numerical expressions into appropriate calculator sequences		
Compare and order rational numbers	Estimation	
Identify alternative representations of rational numbers		
Round whole numbers to a specified place value		
Solve problems using estimation strategies		41, 43
Compare and order rational numbers	Mathematical Connections	2, 3
Identify and use field properties of addition and multiplication		12, 19
Match pictorial models to fraction names and notation		1
Translate between visual representations, sentences, and symbolic notation		
Identify factors or multiples of numbers	Reasoning and Problem Solving	7
Solve problems using numerical reasoning		
Solve problems using appropriate strategies		45, 47, 48, 49
Solve problems using estimations strategies		40, 44
Solve problems using nonroutine strategies		46, 50
Patterns, Relationships, and Algebra		
Solve problems involving patterns	Mathematical Connections	16, 17, 24
Solve problems using ratio or proportion		18
Translate problem situations into algebraic equations and expressions		13
Solve simple algebraic equations	Reasoning and Problem Solving	11
Data, Statistics, and Probability		
Read and interpret tables and graphs	Communication and Representation	23, 26
Read and interpret tables and graphs	Estimation	15
Analyze tables and graphs		
Identify possible outcomes		
Determine and use measures of central tendency	Mathematical Connections	25
Read and interpret tables and graphs		24
Determine combinations and permutations		27
Identify probabilities of simple events	Reasoning and Problem Solving	20

SAT 10 Standards for Grade 7	Process Clusters	Test Items
Geometry and Measurement		
Identify geometric transformations	Mathematical Connections	33
Identify points on a coordinate grid		34
Solve problems using properties of geometric figures		21, 22, 28, 29
Solve problems using spatial reasoning		
Solve problems involving perimeter or area		30, 31, 36
Determine measurements indirectly from scale drawings	Estimation	38, 39
Estimate capacity using customary or metric units		8, 32
Identify appropriate units of measurements		42
Estimate or measure length using customary or metric units	Reasoning and Problem Solving	35
Solve problems involving elapsed time		37
MATHEMATICS: PROCEDURES		
Computation with Whole Numbers		
Addition of whole numbers using symbolic notation		
Addition of whole numbers in context		10, 13
Subtraction of whole numbers using symbolic notation		
Subtraction of whole numbers in context		14, 19
Multiplication of whole numbers using symbolic notation		1, 2
Multiplication of whole numbers in context		9, 12, 19
Division of whole numbers using symbolic notation		3
Division of whole numbers in context		11, 13, 29
Computation with Decimals		
Addition of decimals using symbolic notation		
Addition of decimals in context		17
Subtraction of decimals using symbolic notation		
Subtraction of decimals in context		22, 28
Multiplication of decimals using symbolic notation		4
Multiplication of decimals in context		16, 17, 18
Division of decimals using symbolic notation		7
Division of decimals in context		15, 30
Computation with Fractions		
Addition of fractions using symbolic notation		5
Addition of fractions in context		23, 27
Subtraction of fractions using symbolic notation		8
Subtraction of fractions in context		21
Multiplication of fractions using symbolic notation		6
Multiplication of fractions in context		20, 24, 25, 26

Correlation Chart: Practice Test to the ITBS Standards

ITBS CONCEPT	TEST ITEM(S)
NUMBER PROPERTIES AND OPERATIONS	
Represent numbers	
Apply properties of numbers	30
Classify numbers by divisibility	25
Perform operations	
Write numbers in exponential form	
ALGEBRA	
Use and interpret operational symbols	21
Use and interpret relational symbols	
Solve equations	33
Solve inequalities	
Use expressions to model a situation	19
Understand numerical patterns	20, 26
GEOMETRY	
Identify geometric figures	27
Describe geometric relationships	
Describe geometric patterns	
Apply the concept of area	12, 28, 29
MEASUREMENT	
Measure time	
Use appropriate units	
Identify appropriate units	22
PROBABILITY AND STATISTICS	
Apply counting rules	18
Apply measures of central tendency	32
Understand measures of variability	
ESTIMATION	
Use standard rounding	34, 35, 40
Use order of magnitude	37
Use number sense	36
PROBLEM SOLVING	
Single-step	31
Multiple-step	16, 17
Approaches and procedures	38, 39
DATA INTERPRETATION	
To understand functional relationships	23, 24
To draw conclusions	

ITBS CONCEPT	TEST ITEM(S)
ADD AND SUBTRACT WITH WHOLE NUMBERS	
Add with regrouping	1, 15
Subtract with regrouping	2
MULTIPLY AND DIVIDE WITH WHOLE NUMBERS	
Multiply with regrouping	
Multiply without regrouping	
Divide without a remainder	
Divide with a remainder	
ADD AND SUBTRACT WITH FRACTIONS	
Add fractions with different denominators	5
Subtract fractions with the same denominator	6
Subtract fractions with different denominators	
MULTIPLY AND DIVIDE WITH FRACTIONS	
Multiply a fraction with a whole number	
Multiply two simple fractions	7
Divide a fraction and a whole number	
Divide two simple fractions	8
ADD AND SUBTRACT WITH DECIMALS	
Add decimals with the same number of decimal places	
Add decimals with different numbers of decimal places	9
Subtract decimals with the same number of decimal places	10
MULTIPLY AND DIVIDE WITH DECIMALS	
Multiply a decimal number and a whole number	3, 14
Multiply two decimals	11
Divide decimals with a whole number divisor	4
Divide decimals with decimal divisors	13

Correlation Chart: Practice Test to TerraNova for Grade 7

TERRANOVA OBJECTIVES FOR GRADE 7	TEST ITEM(S)
PARTS 1 AND 2	
10 Number and Number Relations • Demonstrate an understanding of number, number sense, and number theory by ordering numbers, representing numbers in equivalent forms, identifying relationships, interpreting numbers in real-world situations, and applying number concepts in real-world situations.	12, 13, 15, 32, 39
11 Computation and Numerical Estimation • Demonstrate proficiency in computation procedures, solve real-world computation problems, apply a variety of estimation strategies, and determine reasonableness of results.	1, 2, 3, 4, 5, 6, 7, 24, 25, 31, 38
12 Operation Concepts • Demonstrate an understanding of the properties and relationships of operations, relate mathematical representations to problem situations, and apply operational processes to solve problems	10
13 Measurement • Demonstrate an understanding of measurement systems, units, and tools by describing, calculating, or estimating size, location, and time; by using the concepts of perimeter, area, volume, capacity, weight, and mass; and by identifying appropriate degrees of accuracy. • Solve problems involving principles of measurement, rate, and scale.	9, 19, 20, 23, 29, 34, 52, 53
14 Geometry and Spatial Sense • Demonstrate spatial sense and an understanding of geometry by visualizing and identifying two- and three- dimensional objects, classifying shapes, recognizing symmetry, using transformations, applying geometric formulas, and evaluating properties of geometric figures.	8, 14, 21, 22, 40, 50, 51, 54, 55, 56
15 Data Analysis, Statistics and Probability • Analyze, interpret, and evaluate data in various forms; and apply the concepts and processes of data analysis, statistics, and probability to real-world situations.	16, 41, 42, 43, 44, 45, 46, 47, 48, 49
16 Patterns, Functions, Algebra • Recognize and extend patterns. • Demonstrate an understanding of functional relationships, algebraic processes, variables, and inequality. • Recognize algebraic representations of problem situations and apply algebraic methods to solve real-world problems.	11, 18, 27, 28, 30, 33, 35, 36, 37
17 Problem Solving and Reasoning • Select and apply problem-solving strategies, identify necessary information, use patterns and relationships to evaluate situations, apply inductive and deductive reasoning and spatial and proportional reasoning, and solve a variety of non-routine, real-world problems.	17, 26

TERRANOVA OBJECTIVES FOR GRADE 7	TEST ITEM(S)
PART 3	
43 Add Whole Numbers • Add whole numbers.	
44 Subtract Whole Numbers • Subtract whole numbers.	
45 Multiply Whole Numbers • Multiply whole numbers.	
46 Divide Whole Numbers • Divide whole numbers.	
47 Decimals • Add, subtract, multiply, and divide decimals.	1, 4, 6, 7, 10
48 Fractions • Add, subtract, multiply, and divide fractions.	8, 9, 11
49 Integers • Add, subtract, multiply, and divide integers.	2, 12, 14, 16
50 Percents • Solve computational problems involving percents.	3, 17, 18, 20
51 Order of Operations • Solve computational problems involving the standard order of operations.	5, 13, 15, 19
52 Algebraic Operations • Solve computational problems involving exponents, roots, absolute value, and algebraic expressions and equations.	

Answers

Screening Test 1

1. C **2.** B **3.** A **4.** D **5.** C **6.** B **7.** C **8.** A **9.** A **10.** C
11. B **12.** C **13.** D **14.** D **15.** C **16.** D **17.** C **18.** B
19. A **20.** B **21.** C **22.** B **23.** B **24.** C **25.** B **26.** C
27. B **28.** C **29.** C **30.** C **31.** C **32.** B **33.** C **34.** B
35. B **36.** C

Benchmark Test 1

1. D **2.** H **3.** D **4.** G **5.** D **6.** G **7.** D **8.** G **9.** D
10. H **11.** C **12.** J **13.** D **14.** J **15.** B **16.** H **17.** C
18. G **19.** B **20.** G **21.** C **22.** G **23.** C **24.** J **25.** D
26. H **27.** C **28.** F **29.** B **30.** H **31.** C **32.** F **33.** D
34. J **35.** B **36.** H

Benchmark Test 2

1. B **2.** G **3.** A **4.** G **5.** A **6.** G **7.** B **8.** H **9.** C
10. J **11.** D **12.** G **13.** A **14.** G **15.** C **16.** G **17.** A
18. F **19.** D **20.** G **21.** D **22.** J **23.** B **24.** F **25.** A
26. F **27.** A **28.** J **29.** A **30.** H **31.** D **32.** H **33.** C

Benchmark Test 3

1. C **2.** G **3.** C **4.** F **5.** D **6.** G **7.** D **8.** J **9.** B
10. G **11.** B **12.** G **13.** C **14.** J **15.** B **16.** F **17.** D
18. F **19.** C **20.** F **21.** D **22.** H **23.** A **24.** G **25.** C
26. F **27.** D **28.** H **29.** A **30.** H **31.** B **32.** J **33.** A
34. G **35.** D **36.** F

Benchmark Test 4

1. C **2.** F **3.** C **4.** G **5.** D **6.** G **7.** C **8.** F **9.** D
10. F **11.** D **12.** H **13.** D **14.** H **15.** B **16.** H **17.** C
18. J **19.** B **20.** H **21.** B **22.** J **23.** A **24.** H **25.** B
26. H **27.** A **28.** F **29.** C **30.** H **31.** D **32.** F **33.** D
34. J **35.** A **36.** H

Benchmark Test 5

1. C **2.** F **3.** B **4.** H **5.** B **6.** H **7.** C **8.** J **9.** A
10. G **11.** B **12.** F **13.** B **14.** G **15.** D **16.** J **17.** A
18. F **19.** B **20.** G **21.** C **22.** F **23.** A **24.** J **25.** A
26. F **27.** D **28.** G **29.** A **30.** J **31.** C **32.** G **33.** D
34. H **35.** A **36.** J **37.** A **38.** H **39.** C

Quarter 1 Test, Form A

1. 64 **2.** 0.5366 meters **3.** $28.67 **4.** 2,500 cm **5.** 16
6. -3 **7.** -50 meters/minute **8.** $-2, -\frac{7}{8}, \frac{1}{4}, 0.3$ **9.** 675
10. 7.0×10^9 **11.** 90 **12.** $\frac{6}{7}$ **13.** $\frac{8}{11}, \frac{7}{9}, \frac{9}{10}$ **14.** $2\frac{1}{7}$ **15.** 11
16. 77 **17.** The two scores are equal: $\frac{32}{40} = \frac{24}{30} = \frac{4}{5}$ or 80%
18. 4 miles **19.** $\frac{11}{15}$ **20.** $7\frac{1}{3}$ **21.** $7\frac{7}{10}$ **22.** $1\frac{4}{21}$ **23.** 23 yd
24. 16.4 g **25.** 36,000 **26.** $1\frac{1}{2}$ mi **27.** $7\frac{1}{2}$ in. **28.** 24 slices
29. 10 lb 4 oz, or $10\frac{1}{4}$ lb **30.** 15 lb 12 oz **31.** 14.7 in. **32.** 4

Quarter 1 Test, Form B

1. 175 **2.** 1.33 seconds **3.** $19.16 **4.** 0.32 **5.** 21 **6.** 70 points
7. -325 students **8.** $-2, -\frac{1}{2}, 0.5, \frac{2}{3}$ **9.** 70 **10.** 5.96×10^5
11. 84 **12.** $\frac{7}{12}$ **13.** $\frac{5}{6}, \frac{11}{12}, \frac{7}{4}$ **14.** $2\frac{5}{6}$ **15.** 4 tickets **16.** 14
17. Erin: 62.5%, Lauren: 70%. Lauren was more successful.
18. 9 yd **19.** $1\frac{1}{8}$ hours **20.** $17\frac{23}{24}$ **21.** $7\frac{1}{2}$ **22.** $2\frac{1}{5}$ **23.** 6 ft
24. 24.2 mL **25.** 4,100 **26.** $3\frac{1}{8}$ mi **27.** 9 students **28.** 13 stamps
29. 8 ft $\frac{1}{2}$ in. or $8\frac{1}{24}$ ft **30.** Jill is faster. **31.** 19.8 g **32.** 6

Quarter 1 Test, Form D

1. 20 **2.** 1.82 **3.** $28.67 **4.** 2,500 cm **5.** 16 **6.** 7 **7.** 15
8. 675 **9.** 7.0×10^9 **10.** $\frac{6}{7}$ **11.** $\frac{1}{6}, \frac{2}{3}, \frac{3}{4}$ **12.** $2\frac{1}{7}$ **13.** 11
14. 77 **15.** 0.625 **16.** 4 mi **17.** $\frac{11}{15}$ **18.** $7\frac{1}{3}$ **19.** 23 yd
20. 16.4 g **21.** 36,000 **22.** $7\frac{1}{2}$ in. **23.** 24 slices **24.** $9\frac{1}{2}$ lb

Quarter 1 Test, Form E

1. 50 **2.** 3.84 **3.** $19.16 **4.** 0.32 **5.** 21 **6.** -6 **7.** -22
8. 70 **9.** 5.96×10^5 **10.** $\frac{7}{12}$ **11.** $\frac{5}{6}, \frac{11}{12}, \frac{7}{4}$ **12.** $2\frac{5}{6}$ **13.** 4 tickets
14. 14 **15.** 0.875 **16.** 9 yd **17.** $1\frac{1}{8}$ hours **18.** $17\frac{23}{24}$ **19.** 6 ft
20. 24.2 mL **21.** 4,100 **22.** 13 stamps **23.** 9 students **24.** 19.76 g

Quarter 2 Test, Form A

1. $d = 13$ **2.** $p = 105$ **3.** $x = -40$ **4.** $x - 0.06 = 59.60; x = 59.66$
5. $15l = 60; l = 4$ **6.** Subtract 11 from both sides and then
divide each side by 3. **7.** $0.79p + 3.98 = 7.93$ **8.** Sample
answer: x divided by four, increased by 5 **9.** $x \leq -3$ **10.** $x \geq 7.255$
11. $m > -30$ **12.** $24 : 18; \frac{24}{18}$ **13.** $4 \frac{\text{passes}}{\text{completion}}$ **14.** 256 points
15. no: $\frac{12,000}{8} = \frac{1,500}{1}; \frac{8,000}{5} = \frac{1,600}{1}$ **16.** $x = 4$ **17.** 75 ft
18. 1 in. = 5 miles **19.** 2.3% **20.** 0.4 **21.** 140% **22.** $\frac{47}{100}$
23. $33\frac{1}{3}$% **24.** 980 **25.** 569 **26.** $61.56 **27.** 14% **28.** $x = 28$
29. 80 **30.** Sample answer: A scale drawing is an enlarged or
reduced drawing of an object that is similar to the actual object.
31. $12p + 750 = $2,250; p = 125 **32.** $466

Quarter 2 Test, Form B

1. $e = 13.9$ **2.** $t = 17.2$ **3.** $x = -\frac{1}{3}$ **4.** $x + 2 = 16.5; x = 14.5$ ft
5. $5x = $30; x = 6$ hr **6.** Sample answer: Subtract 3 from both
sides of the equation. Then multiply both sides by 4. **7.** $1.19 +$
$0.3x = 2.99; x = 6$ juice boxes **8.** 2 times a number, decreased
by 5 **9.** $x \geq -1$ **10.** $x \leq 5.6$ **11.** $m < -40$ **12.** $16 : 14; \frac{16}{14}$
13. $4 \frac{\text{pitches}}{\text{foul ball}}$ **14.** 48 **15.** no; $\frac{11}{12,000} \neq \frac{9}{9,000}$ **16.** $x = 18$
17. 225 ft **18.** 1 in. = 5 mi **19.** 5.8% **20.** 0.72 **21.** 112.5%
22. $\frac{7}{20}$ **23.** 25% **24.** $400 **25.** 452 **26.** $95 skis on sale for
10% off ($85.50 < $90.00) **27.** 25% increase **28.** $x = 45$
29. $25,000 **30.** Sample answer: A scale is the ratio that
compares a length in a drawing to the corresponding length in
the actual object. **31.** $24p + 300 = 2,100; p = 75 **32.** $442.40

Answers (continued)

Quarter 2 Test, Form D

1. $d = 13$ **2.** $15l = 60; l = 4$ **3.** Subtract 11 from both sides and then divide each side by 3. **4.** $0.79p + 3.98 = 7.93$ **5.** $\frac{m}{4}$ **6.** $x < -3$ **7.** $x \geq 7.25$ **8.** $m > -30$ **9.** $24 : 18; \frac{24}{18}$ **10.** $4 \frac{\text{passes}}{\text{completion}}$ **11.** 256 points **12.** no **13.** $x = 4$ **14.** 75 ft **15.** 1 in. = 5 mi **16.** 2.3% **17.** 0.4 **18.** 140% **19.** $\frac{47}{100}$ **20.** $33\frac{1}{3}\%$ **21.** 980 **22.** \$61.56 **23.** 15.8% **24.** 25% **25.** \$66

Quarter 2 Test, Form E

1. $e = 13.9$ **2.** $5x = \$30; x = 6$ hr **3.** Sample answer: Subtract 3 from both sides of the equation. Then multiply both sides by 4. **4.** $1.19 + 0.3x = 2.99; x = 6$ juice boxes **5.** $x + 10$ **6.** $x \geq -1$ **7.** $x \leq 5.6$ **8.** $m < -40$ **9.** $16 : 14; \frac{16}{14}$ **10.** $4 \frac{\text{pitches}}{\text{foul ball}}$ **11.** 48 **12.** yes **13.** $x = 18$ **14.** 225 ft **15.** 1 in. = 5 mi **16.** 5.8% **17.** 0.72 **18.** 112.5% **19.** $\frac{7}{20}$ **20.** 25% **21.** \$400 **22.** \$95 skis on sale for 10% off (\$85.50 < \$90.00) **23.** 32% increase **24.** 25% **25.** \$92.40

Quarter 3 Test, Form A

1.

2. acute **3.** 61° **4.** D is the midpoint of $\overline{LM}$. **5.** right, obtuse, acute **6.** 58° **7.** hexagon **8a.** FDE **8b.** DEF **9.** $\overline{RT}$ **10.** 43.4% **11.** 10.07 cm² **12.** 162 in.² **13.** 14 **14.** 15 **15.** rectangular prism **16.** 1,350 m² **17.** $-243,729$ **18.** \$4.76, \$5.95 **19.** $f(n) = n^2$ **20.** \$306.31 **21.** $a = 4(c + b)$ **22.** 8 cm² **23.** 240 in.³ **24.** 90°, 48° **25.** parallelogram **26.** $C = 84.8$ ft; $A = 572.3$ ft

Quarter 3 Test, Form B

1.
2. obtuse **3.** 151° **4.** $\overline{AC}, \overline{GE}, \overline{DB}$ **5.** scalene, equilateral, isosceles **6.** 86° **7.** octagon **8a.** Q **8b.** R **9.** $\overline{XT}, \overline{XR}, \overline{TS}, \overline{RT},$ or $\overline{RS}$ **10.** \$510 **11.** 999 m² **12.** 110 dm² **13.** 12 **14.** 24 **15.** cone **16.** 132 ft² **17.** 12.5, 6.25 **18.** \$19.96, \$24.95 **19.** $f(n) = n^3$ **20.** \$552.90 **21.** $\frac{A}{2\pi} = r$ **22.** 16 cm² **23.** 1,260 in.³ **24.** 39° and 39° **25.** square, rectangle, rhombus, parallelogram **26.** $C = 201.0$ ft; $A = 3,215.4$ ft²

Quarter 3 Test, Form D

1.
2. acute **3.** 60° **4.** D is the midpoint of $\overline{LM}$. **5.** right **6.** 58° **7.** hexagon **8a.** FDE **8b.** DEF **9.** $\overline{RT}$ **10.** 17% **11.** 162 in.² **12.** 10 **13.** 19.2 **14.** rectangular prism **15.** 204 m² **16.** 40, 48 **17.** \$4.76, \$5.95 **18.** $f(n) = n + 9$ **19.** \$75 **20.** $a = 4(c + b)$ **21.** 8 cm² **22.** 240 in.³ **23.** $C = 31.4$ ft; $A = 78.5$ ft

Quarter 3 Test, Form E

1.

2. obtuse **3.** 150° **4.** $\overline{AC}, \overline{GE},$ or $\overline{DB}$ **5.** isosceles **6.** 86° **7.** octagon **8a.** Q **8b.** R **9.** $\overline{XT}, \overline{XR}, \overline{TS}, \overline{RT},$ or $\overline{RS}$ **10.** \$510 **11.** 999 m² **12.** 110 dm² **13.** 9 **14.** 12 **15.** cone **16.** 132 ft² **17.** 36, 49 **18.** \$19.96, \$24.95 **19.** $f(n) = 4n$ **20.** \$48 **21.** $\frac{A}{2\pi} = r$ **22.** 16 cm² **23.** 1,050 in.³ **24.** $C = 188.4$ ft; $A = 2,826$ ft²

Quarter 4 Test, Form A

1. Quadrant II **2.** Sample answer: $(-3, -1)$ **3.** $y = -2x + 1$, because the slope is negative **4.** point D **5.** $y = |x - 4|$ **6.** $(1, 2)$ **7.** $(5, -5)$ **8.** 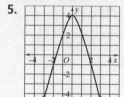 **9.** 90° or $\frac{1}{4}$ turn **10.** \$110 **11.** $\frac{99}{436} = \frac{1,151}{x}; x = 5,069$ fish **12.** $\frac{1}{4}$ **13.** $\frac{2}{5}$ **14.** $\frac{1}{64}$ **15.** 840 **16.** 6 **17.** 2 **18.** 120 **19.** 20 **20.** Sample answer: a; walking through the halls of a school, you are more likely to get a larger and more varied sample of students; not all students will use one particular entrance. **21.** mean, highest; mode, lowest; answers will vary **22.** Sample answer: should include 3 units per interval to accommodate a data range of 21

Quarter 4 Test, Form B

1. Quadrant III **2.** no **3.** $y = -5x - 1$ because the slope is negative **4.** point G **5.**

6. $(1, -5)$

7. $(4, -3)$ **8.**  **9.** 180° or $\frac{1}{2}$ turn **10.** 792 **11.** $\frac{50}{70} = \frac{436}{x}; x = 610$ birds **12.** $\frac{3}{4}$ **13.** $\frac{9}{16}$ **14.** $\frac{7}{30}$ **15.** 120 **16.** 720 **17.** 9 **18.** 30 **19.** 72 **20.** Sample answer: b. Standing in front of the library from open to close, you are more likely to get a larger and varied sample. More students (nonvoters) might visit the library during the hours of 4–6 P.M. **21.** median, highest; mode, lowest; answers will vary. **22.** Sample answer: The line plot shows 28 responses from only 24 students. It is likely that some students participated in more than one sport.

Answers (continued)

Quarter 4 Test, Form D

1. Quadrant II **2.** Sample answer: $(-3, -1)$ **3.** $y = -2x + 1$, because the slope is negative **4.** $y = |x - 4|$ **5.** $(1, 2)$

6. 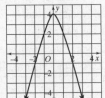 **7.** $90°$ or $\frac{1}{4}$ turn **8.** $110

9. $\frac{99}{436} = \frac{1,151}{x}$; $x = 5,069$ fish **10.** $\frac{2}{5}$ **11.** $\frac{1}{64}$ **12.** $840

13. 2 **14.** 120 **15.** Sample answer: a; walking through the halls of a school, you are more likely to get a larger and more varied sample of students; not all students will use one particular entrance. **16.** mean, highest; mode, lowest; answers will vary **17.** Sample answer: should include 3 units per interval to accommodate a data range of 21

Quarter 4 Test, Form E

1. Quadrant III **2.** no **3.** $y = -5x - 1$ because the slope is negative **4.**

5. $(1, -5)$

6. **7.** $180°$ or $\frac{1}{2}$ turn **8.** 792

9. $\frac{50}{70} = \frac{436}{x}$; $x = 610$ birds **10.** $\frac{3}{4}$ **11.** $\frac{7}{30}$ **12.** 720

13. 9 **14.** 30 **15.** Sample answer: b. Standing in front of the library from open to close, you are more likely to get a larger and varied sample. More students (nonvoters) might visit the library during the hours of 4–6 P.M. **16.** median, highest; mode, lowest; answers will vary. **17.** Sample answer: The line plot shows 28 responses from only 24 students. It is likely that some students participated in more than one sport.

Mid-Course Test, Form A

1. $31 **2.** $18.70 **3.** $34.02 **4.** 4.052 kg **5.** $-13, -1, 3, 17, 19$ **6.** 14,397 ft **7.** $-$2,250 **8.** 53,000 ft^2 **9.** 11 **10.** 5 **11.** 50 **12.** 24 **13.** $55 + 42 + m = 155$; 58 mice **14.** The number is negative since a positive times a negative is a negative. **15.** $3x + 6$ **16.** $y = -6$ **17.** $x = 24$ **18.** 420 calories **19.** $x < 7$ or $7 > x$ **20.** $t \le 28$ **21.** $t > 1201$ **22.** 6 **23.** 5,930 **24.** 12 **25.** $\frac{1}{2}$ **26.** Liz **27.** 40 **28.** $\frac{20}{3}$ **29.** $-1, \frac{-2}{3}, \frac{1}{8}, 0.3$ **30.** $\frac{1}{6}$ cup **31.** $\frac{3}{8}$ pound **32.** $4\frac{1}{6}$ cup **33.** about 260 nails **34.** $\frac{1}{6}$ **35.** 3:30 P.M. **36.** 30 **37.** centimeter **38.** 5 to 9, 5 : 9, $\frac{5}{9}$ **39.** 1.7 **40.** 3 cans for $2 **41.** $\frac{2}{5}$ **42.** 10 hours **43.** 360 km **44.** 20% **45.** $\frac{2}{5}, 0.53, \frac{7}{12}, 72\%$ **46.** 40% **47.** 4% **48.** 144 **49.** 21 **50.** $4\frac{1}{4}$ **51.** 21.6 **52.** Sample answer: -8 and 104.

53. 8.49×10^4 miles **54.** Yes; the number formed by the last three digits (640) is divisible by 8, so the number is divisible by 8. **55.** $2,976.80 **56.** 66% **57a.** $6\frac{1}{4}$ hours **57b.** Answers will vary. Sample: about $250 **58.** Yes; there will be $24.20 extra.

Mid-Course Test, Form B

1. 102 **2.** $48.70 **3.** 76.5 pounds **4.** 3,260 g **5.** $-12, -2, 4, 16, 20$ **6.** 7 yard loss **7.** 20 seconds **8.** 161 in.^{2} **9.** 16 **10.** 14 **11.** 4 **12.** 192 **13.** $x + 975 = 1,500$; 525 m^3 **14.** Stuart divided -100 by 5 when he should have multiplied 5 by -100 to get $x = -500$. **15.** $\frac{n}{4} - 10$ **16.** $y = 4$ **17.** $x = 20$ **18.** 980 calories **19.** $7 \le y$ or $y \ge 7$ **20.** $n \ge 2$ **21.** $y \le 7$ **22.** 33 **23.** 82,700 **24.** 15 **25.** $\frac{2}{5}$ **26.** 72 m^2 **27.** $\frac{25}{7}$ **28.** $-2, \frac{-3}{4}, 0.6, \frac{2}{3}$ **29.** $1\frac{5}{8}$ yd **30.** $6\frac{1}{6}$ cups **31.** $\frac{1}{2}$ cup **32.** 17 blocks **33.** $\frac{26}{55}$ **34.** 2:00 P.M. **35.** 1 lb 3 oz **36.** fluid ounce **37.** 9:20, 9 to 20, or $\frac{9}{20}$ **38.** 0.6 **39.** $2.95 **40.** 50 for $3.25 **41.** $\frac{3}{10}$ **42.** 20 months **43.** 132 feet **44.** 70% **45.** 81%, $\frac{11}{13}, \frac{6}{7}, 0.89$ **46.** 27.8% **47.** $75,000 **48.** 61 **49.** 8 **50.** 3 **51.** 7 **52.** Sample answer: $-2, 15, 40$ **53.** Pacific, 6.41863×10^7 mi^2, Atlantic, 3.342×10^7 mi^2 **54.** Yes, 8,592 is divisible by 3 since the sum of the digits 8, 5, 9, and 2 is divisible by 3. **55.** $1,170.40 **56.** $29.40 **57a.** $7\frac{1}{4}$ hours **57b.** Answers will vary. Sample: about $315. **58.** No; she will have to pay $12.00 extra.

Mid-Course Test, Form D

1. $31 **2.** $18.70 **3.** $34.02 **4.** 4.052 kg **5.** $-13, -1, 3, 17, 19$ **6.** 14,397 ft **7.** $-$2,250 **8.** 11 **9.** 5 **10.** 50 **11.** 24 **12.** The number is negative since a positive times a negative is a negative. **13.** $3x + 6$ **14.** $y = -6$ **15.** $x = 24$ **16.** $x < 7$ or $7 > x$ **17.** $t \le 28$ **18.** $t > 120$ **19.** 6 **20.** 5,930 **21.** 12 **22.** $\frac{1}{2}$ **23.** 40 **24.** $\frac{20}{3}$ **25.** $-1, \frac{-2}{3}, \frac{1}{8}, 0.3$ **26.** $7\frac{1}{2}$ **27.** $\frac{1}{6}$ cup **28.** $\frac{3}{8}$ pound **29.** $2\frac{1}{2} \times 1\frac{2}{3} = 4\frac{1}{6}$ cup **30.** about 260 nails **31.** $\frac{1}{6}$ **32.** 3:30 P.M. **33.** 30 **34.** centimeter **35.** 5 to 9, 5:9, $\frac{5}{9}$ **36.** 3 cans for $2 **37.** $\frac{2}{5}$ **38.** 10 hours **39.** 360 km **40.** 20% **41.** $\frac{2}{5}, 0.53, \frac{7}{12}, 72\%$ **42.** 40% **43.** 4% **44.** 144 **45.** 21 **46.** $4\frac{1}{4}$ **47.** 21.6 **48.** 1.6 **49.** Yes; the number formed by the last three digits (640) is divisible by 8, so the number is divisible by 8. **50.** $2,976.80 **51a.** $6\frac{1}{4}$ hours **51b.** Answers will vary. Sample: about $250 **52.** Yes; there will be $24.20 extra.

Answers (continued)

Mid-Course Test, Form E

1. 102 **2.** $48.70 **3.** 76.5 pounds **4.** 3,260 g **5.** $-12, -2,$
$4, 16, 20$ **6.** 7 yard loss **7.** 161 in.^{2} **8.** 16 **9.** 14 **10.** 4
11. 192 **12.** Stuart divided -100 by 5 when he should have
multiplied 5 by -100 to get $x = -500$. **13.** $\frac{n}{4} - 10$
14. $y = 4$ **15.** $x = 20$ **16.** $7 \leq y$ or $y \geq 7$ **17.** $n \geq 2$
18. $y \leq 7$ **19.** 33 **20.** 82,700 **21.** 15 **22.** $\frac{2}{5}$ **23.** 72 m^2
24. $\frac{25}{7}$ **25.** $-2, \frac{-3}{4}, 0.6, \frac{2}{3}$ **26.** 8 **27.** $1\frac{5}{8}$ yd **28.** $6\frac{1}{6}$ cups
29. $\frac{1}{2}$ cup **30.** 17 blocks **31.** $\frac{26}{55}$ **32.** 2:00 P.M. **33.** 1 lb 3 oz
34. fluid ounce **35.** 9:20, 9 to 20, or $\frac{9}{20}$ **36.** 50 for $3.25
37. $\frac{3}{10}$ **38.** 20 months **39.** 132 feet **40.** 70% **41.** 81%,
$\frac{11}{13}, \frac{6}{7}, 0.89$ **42.** 27.8% **43.** 61 **44.** 8 **45.** 3 **46.** 7
47. 15 **48.** Pacific, 6.41863×10^7 mi^2; Atlantic, 3.342×10^7 mi^2
49. Yes, 8,592 is divisible by 3 since the sum of the digits $8, 5, 9,$
and 2 is divisible by 3. **50.** $1,170.40 **51a.** $7\frac{1}{4}$
51b. Answers will vary. Sample: about $315. **52.** No; she will
have to pay $12.00 extra.

Final Test, Form A

1. 8 **2.** $2.20 **3.** $143.64 **4.** 5 yard loss **5.** $20, 0, -11, -12$
6. 20 weeks **7.** $r = 24$ **8.** Three times a number is negative
twenty-seven. **9.** $x > -4$![number line $-5-4-3-2-1\,0\,1\,2\,3\,4$]
10. $x \leq -3$ **11.** $\frac{8}{9}$ **12.** 21 **13.** $0.\overline{6} < 0.75$
14. $2 \times 3^2 \times 7$ **15.** $15\frac{9}{20}$ miles **16.** 28 oz **17.** $2\frac{1}{8}$ oz **18.** $\frac{1}{12}$
19. 5 lb 4 oz **20.** 16 to 11, 16:11, $\frac{16}{11}$ **21.** 365 mi^2 per county
22. $19.60 for 8 cans of chili **23.** yes; $\frac{55}{95} = \frac{55}{95}$ **24.** 10.5
25. 72%, $\frac{11}{15}, \frac{7}{9}, 0.79$ **26.** 0.009, $\frac{9}{1000}$ **27.** 66% **28.** 268
29. $92.98 **30.** 90 ft^2 **31a.** Sample answer: $\angle 13$ and $\angle 14$ or
$\angle 16$ and $\angle 17$ **31b.** $\overleftrightarrow{GH}$ **31c.** $\overleftrightarrow{AB} \| \overleftrightarrow{EF}$ **32.** isosceles
obtuse **33.** 30° **34.** 288° **35.** 480 cm^2 **36.** 12 in.
37. 1,846 ft^3 **38.** 2,232 m^2 **39.** 5.3 cm **40.** Sample
answer: They both have one base. The base of a cone is a circle.
The base of a pyramid is a polygon. **41.** $-3, -2, -1$
42. Sample answer: gas level in a fuel tank during a trip
43. whale: $d = 20t$; barracuda: $d = 30t$ **44.** $140.71
45. Quadrant III

46.

x	1	2	3	4	5
y	$0.75	$1.50	$2.25	$3.00	$3.75

47. $\frac{1}{4}$ **48.** $y = |x - 3|$ **49.** $(3, -2)$ **50.** 21, 22, 22, 22, 23, 23,
24, 26, 29, 29 **51.** There are 60 more fiction texts in the library
at School C. **52.** a double bar graph **53.** 92.5 **54.** $\frac{8}{25}$

Final Test, Form B

1. 12 **2.** $38.78 **3.** $94.35 **4.** 925 m **5.** $-17, -15, 5, 30$
6. 8 days **7.** $j = -6$ **8.** Four less than a number is negative
three. **9.** $x \leq -1$![number line $-3-2-1\,0\,1\,2$] **10.** $x > 2$
11. $\frac{2}{3}$ **12.** 87 **13.** $\frac{20}{24} < \frac{21}{24}$ **14.** $2 \times 3^2 \times 7$ **15.** $7\frac{3}{4}$ yards
16. 1,050 cards **17.** 6 boards **18.** 8 friends
19. 29 yards 1 foot **20.** 14 to 19, 14:19, $\frac{14}{19}$ **21.** $4\frac{ft}{sec}$
22. 36-ounce bag **23.** no; $\frac{42}{56} \neq \frac{48}{56}$ **24.** 12 **25.** 0.39, $\frac{2}{5}$,
42%, $\frac{11}{24}$ **26.** 1.20, $1\frac{1}{5}$ **27.** 42.3% **28.** 800 **29.** $15.34
30. 64 cm^2 **31a.** Sample answer: $\overleftrightarrow{AB} \perp \overleftrightarrow{IJ}$ **31b.** $\overleftrightarrow{AB} \| \overleftrightarrow{EF}$
31c. Sample answer: $\angle 1$ and $\angle 2$ **32.** equilateral, acute **33.** 23
cm **34.** 144° each for roses and grasses; 72° for pansies **35.** 432
m^2 **36.** 26 feet **37.** 5,319 ft^3 **38.** 90 m^3 **39.** 121 in.^{2}
40. Sample answer: They both have faces that are polygons.
A prism has two parallel bases, a pyramid has only one base.
41. 3, 5, 9 **42.** Sample answer: body temperature of person with a
fever after taking medicine **43.** The barracuda would have
traveled a distance of 180 miles. It would take a whale 9 hours to
travel the same distance. **44.** $12.30 **45.** Quadrant II

46.

x	1	2	3	4	5
y	$2.25	$4.50	$6.75	$9.00	$11.25

47. $-\frac{1}{2}$ **48.** $y = |x - 4|$ **49.** $(-6, 0)$ **50.** 3 **51.** page 4
52. double line graph **53.** 100 **54.** $\frac{7}{10}$, 70%, 0.7

Final Test, Form D

1. 8 **2.** $2.20 **3.** $143.64 **4.** 5 yard loss **5.** $20, 0, -11, -12$
6. $r = 24$ **7.** $x > -4$![number line $-5-4-3-2-1\,0\,1\,2\,3\,4$]
8. $x \leq -3$ **9.** $\frac{8}{9}$ **10.** 21 **11.** $0.\overline{6} < 0.75$ **12.** $2 \times 3^2 \times 7$
13. $15\frac{9}{20}$ miles **14.** 28 oz **15.** $2\frac{1}{8}$ oz **16.** $\frac{1}{12}$ **17.** 5 lb 4 oz
18. 16 to 11, 16 : 11, $\frac{16}{11}$ **19.** $19.60 for 8 cans of chili
20. yes; $\frac{55}{95} = \frac{55}{95}$ **21.** 10.5 **22.** 72%, $\frac{11}{15}, \frac{7}{9}, 0.79$ **23.** 0.009,
$\frac{9}{1000}$ **24.** 66% **25.** 268 **26.** $92.98 **27a.** Sample answer:
$\angle 13$ and $\angle 14$ or $\angle 16$ and $\angle 17$ **27b.** $\overleftrightarrow{GH}$ **27c.** $\overleftrightarrow{AB} \| \overleftrightarrow{EF}$
28. isosceles, obtuse **29.** 30° **30.** 288° **31.** 480 cm^2
32. 12 in. **33.** 1,846 ft^3 **34.** 2,232 m^2 **35.** Sample answer:
They both have a vertex and a base. A cone has a curved
surface; all the surfaces of a pyramid are polygons. **36.** $-3, -2, -1$
37. whale: $d = 20t$; barracuda: $d = 30t$ **38.** $140.71
39. Quadrant III **40.** $\frac{1}{4}$ **41.** $y = |x - 3|$ **42.** $(3, -2)$
43. 21, 22, 22, 22, 23, 23, 24, 26, 29, 29 **44.** There are 60 more
fiction texts in the library at School C. **45.** 92.5 **46.** $\frac{8}{25}$

Answers (continued)

Final Test, Form E

1. 12   **2.** $38.78   **3.** $94.35   **4.** 925 m   **5.** $-17, -15, 5, 30$

6. $j = -6$ **7.** $x \le -1$ **8.** $x > 2$

9. $\frac{2}{3}$ **10.** 87   **11.** $\frac{20}{24} < \frac{21}{24}$ **12.** $2^2 \times 5 \times 11$ **13.** $7\frac{3}{4}$ yards

14. 1,050 cards   **15.** 6 boards   **16.** 8 friends   **17.** 29 yards 1 foot

18. 14 to 19, 14 : 19, $\frac{14}{19}$ **19.** 36-ounce bag   **20.** no; $\frac{42}{56} \ne \frac{48}{56}$

21. 12   **22.** $0.39, \frac{2}{5}, 42\%, \frac{11}{24}$ **23.** $1.20, 1\frac{1}{5}$ **24.** 40%

25. 800   **26.** $15.34   **27a.** Sample answer: $\overleftrightarrow{AB} \perp \overleftrightarrow{IJ}$

27b. $\overleftrightarrow{AB} \| \overleftrightarrow{EF}$ **27c.** Sample answer: $\angle 1$ and $\angle 2$

28. equilateral, acute   **29.** 23 cm   **30.** 144° each for roses and grasses; 72° for pansies   **31.** 432 m^2 **32.** 26 feet   **33.** 5,319 ft^3

34. 90 m^3 **35.** Sample answer: They both have faces that are polygons. A prism has two parallel bases, a pyramid has only one base.   **36.** 3, 5, 9   **37.** The barracuda would have traveled a distance of 180 miles. It would take a whale 9 hours to travel the same distance.   **38.** $12.30   **39.** Quadrant II   **40.** $-\frac{1}{2}$

41. $y = |x - 4|$ **42.** $(-6, 0)$ **43.** 3   **44.** page 4   **45.** 100

46. $\frac{7}{10}, 70\%, 0.7$

Answers (continued)

Test-Taking Strategies

Writing Gridded Responses
1. 28.8 **2.** 12.66 **3.** 57.66 **4.** 10.2 **5.** 2.4 or $\frac{12}{5}$ **6.** 2
7. 5 **8.** 48 **9.** 80 **10.** 372 **11.** 150 **12.** 8 **13.** 12.06
14. 465 **15.** 15

Writing Short Responses
1a. Sample answer: 2 points: The equation and the
solution are correct. 1 point: The equation is correct but
there is an arithmetic error. 0 points: There is no work
shown and the solution is incorrect. **1b.** Sample answer:
$\frac{8.75 - 2.75}{1.5} = 4$ games. **2.** Sample answer: Let $t =$ the
number of T-shirts. $6.99t + 21.99 = 63.93$; $6.99t = 41.94$;
$\frac{6.99t}{6.99} = \frac{41.94}{6.99}$; $t = 6$; Marcus bought 6 T-shirts.

Reading for Understanding
1. 310 feet **2.** 140 seconds **3.** 1,584 passengers
4. 1.25 miles **5.** 4,180 lb **6.** Less than 950 kg
7. 14 km or 8.75 mi

Writing Extended Responses
1a. The student added 115.95 to the right side of the
equation instead of subtracting. All other work is done
correctly. **1b.** Sample answer: $42h = \$241.95$;
$h = 5.76$ hours **2a.** Sample answer: The GCF of 256
and 96 is 32, so Aaron can make 32 bags. The number
of purple beads in each bag is $256 \div 32 = 8$; the number of orange beads is $96 \div 21 = 3$. **2b.** Sample
answer: There should be 16 bags.

Using a Variable
1. $5\frac{1}{4}$ pounds **2.** 320 kg **3.** 9,741 flashlights
4. $291.84 **5.** 30 boxes **6.** $265.50 **7.** 120 square feet
8. 18 defective chips **9.** 680 pounds **10.** 52.5 pounds

Working Backward
1. C **2.** G **3** C **4.** G **5.** D **6.** H **7.** B **8.** G **9.** D
10. F **11.** D

Drawing a Picture
1. 35° **2.** Town J **3.** 24° **4.** 4 meters **5.** −2.2
6. isosceles **7.** 16 blocks due west **8.** 9
9. 238 square units

Measuring to Solve
1. $r = 3.5$ cm; $C = 21.98$ cm **2.** $l = 5$ cm, $w = 2.5$ cm; P
$= 15$ cm **3.** $s = 5.5$ cm; $A = 30.25$ cm^2

Estimating the Answer
1. A **2.** G **3.** B **4.** H **5.** B **6.** G **7.** C **8.** J

Answering the Question Asked
1. A **2.** J **3.** A **4.** G **5.** A **6.** J **7.** C

Interpreting Data
1. C **2.** H **3.** C **4.** H

Eliminating Answers
1a. Percent means per hundred, and $\frac{40}{1,000}$ would be less
than 400%, or 40%. **1b.** D **2a.** The denominator needs
to be a factor of 30, and 8 is not. Also, since the apples
are not all the same color, the probability cannot be 1.
2b. H **3a.** The events are independent. You would
multiply the probability of each letter selection: 26
times 26 will be greater than 2 and 26. **3b.** D **4a.** The
number of permutations is $_5P_3 = \frac{5!}{2!}$. The answer must
be less than 5!, which is 120. **4b.** H

Answers: NAEP Practice Test

Multiple Choice

1. B
2. D
3. C
4. D
5. C
6. A
7. D
8. C
9. A
10. B
11. D
12. C
13. E
14. B
15. A
16. B
17. E
18. D
19. E
20. C
21. E
22. B
23. C
24. C
25. C
26. B
27. D
28. B
29. D
30. A
31. C
32. D
33. C
34. C
35. D
36. D
37. B
38. E
39. E
40. B
41. D
42. C
43. B
44. D
45. A
46. B
47. D

48. D
49. B
50. E
51. C
52. A
53. B
54. B
55. C
56. C
57. E
58. B
59. B
60. D
61. A
62. C
63. C

Short Constructed Response

64. Sample answers: Draw out all 15 terms; follow the pattern that each term increases by consecutive numbers; find a formula for the nth term; It would be much easier to use the formula to find the 100th term because adding the consecutive numbers from 1 to 100 is cumbersome and leaves room for error; 5,050.

65. Mary starts off on the treadmill walking at a constant speed

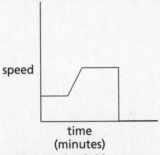

so the graph of this segment should be horizontal since she is not increasing her speed, only her time. Then, her speed does increase for two minutes, so the segment that reflects this increase in speed should be drawn with a positive slope. She then keeps a constant running speed for six minutes, so the graph of this segment should be horizontal and higher on the y-axis since she is now running instead of walking. Since the tread-

mill then suddenly stops, the segment that represents this part of the graph should be a vertical line straight down to 0 on the x-axis.

66. Container A has a surface area of 2,110.08 square inches and would cost $1,055.04 to make.

Container B has a surface area of 864 square inches and would cost $432 to make.

Container C has a surface area of 728 square inches and would cost $364 to make.

The C.E.O. should choose Container C in order to save money.

Extended Constructed Response

67. 7 feet is the greatest length that a segment of fence can be; 22 segments to build the fence around the garden.

68. Since Panther got the most votes, this should be the mascot that the school should choose.

69. Since $x > 0$ and $y > 0$, this means that x and y both must be positive numbers. Since x is smaller than y and you multiply each number by itself, x times, x will still be smaller than y times y. Therefore, $x^2 < y^2$ is a true inequality.

70. $1.87

Answers: SAT 10 Practice Test

Problem Solving

1.	C
2.	F
3.	D
4.	H
5.	C
6.	J
7.	D
8.	J
9.	B
10.	G
11.	C
12.	F
13.	C
14.	H
15.	B
16.	J
17.	A
18.	G
19.	B
20.	H
21.	D
22.	G
23.	C
24.	H
25.	B
26.	J
27.	D
28.	G
29.	C
30.	H
31.	B
32.	H
33.	C
34.	F
35.	C
36.	G
37.	B
38.	H
39.	C
40.	H
41.	B
42.	H
43.	B
44.	H
45.	B
46.	H
47.	A
48.	G
49.	A
50.	J

Procedures

1.	E
2.	G
3.	B
4.	H
5.	C
6.	H
7.	C
8.	G
9.	B
10.	G
11.	A
12.	F
13.	C
14.	K
15.	C
16.	F
17.	E
18.	G
19.	B
20.	G
21.	C
22.	H
23.	A
24.	H
25.	B
26.	H
27.	D
28.	H
29.	C
30.	J

Answers: ITBS Practice Test

1. A
2. F
3. B
4. F
5. C
6. H
7. D
8. J
9. D
10. J
11. C
12. G
13. D
14. G
15. B
16. G
17. A
18. F
19. B
20. G
21. D
22. J
23. D
24. J
25. A
26. F
27. D
28. F
29. B
30. G
31. A
32. H
33. D
34. J
35. D
36. F
37. A
38. G
39. D
40. F

Answers: TerraNova Practice Test

Part 1
1. B
2. F
3. C
4. J
5. C
6. H
7. B
8. F
9. D
10. J
11. B
12. H
13. A
14. G
15. A
16. J
17. C

Part 2
18. F
19. C
20. G
21. B
22. H
23. A
24. J
25. C
26. H
27. C
28. G
29. D
30. J
31. D
32. G
33. C
34. F
35. C
36. J
37. A
38. H
39. C
40. F
41. D
42. G
43. D
44. H
45. B

46. F
47. D
48. G
49. C
50. J
51. A
52. J
53. B
54. J
55. C
56. H

Part 3
1. E
2. J
3. E
4. H
5. C
6. J
7. A
8. H
9. C
10. J
11. B
12. J
13. B
14. G
15. C
16. G
17. E
18. H
19. A
20. G

Answer Sheet

1.	Ⓐ	Ⓑ	Ⓒ	Ⓓ		27.	Ⓐ	Ⓑ	Ⓒ	Ⓓ
2.	Ⓕ	Ⓖ	Ⓗ	Ⓙ		28.	Ⓕ	Ⓖ	Ⓗ	Ⓙ
3.	Ⓐ	Ⓑ	Ⓒ	Ⓓ		29.	Ⓐ	Ⓑ	Ⓒ	Ⓓ
4.	Ⓕ	Ⓖ	Ⓗ	Ⓙ		30.	Ⓕ	Ⓖ	Ⓗ	Ⓙ
5.	Ⓐ	Ⓑ	Ⓒ	Ⓓ		31.	Ⓐ	Ⓑ	Ⓒ	Ⓓ
6.	Ⓕ	Ⓖ	Ⓗ	Ⓙ		32.	Ⓕ	Ⓖ	Ⓗ	Ⓙ
7.	Ⓐ	Ⓑ	Ⓒ	Ⓓ		33.	Ⓐ	Ⓑ	Ⓒ	Ⓓ
8.	Ⓕ	Ⓖ	Ⓗ	Ⓙ		34.	Ⓕ	Ⓖ	Ⓗ	Ⓙ
9.	Ⓐ	Ⓑ	Ⓒ	Ⓓ		35.	Ⓐ	Ⓑ	Ⓒ	Ⓓ
10.	Ⓕ	Ⓖ	Ⓗ	Ⓙ		36.	Ⓕ	Ⓖ	Ⓗ	Ⓙ
11.	Ⓐ	Ⓑ	Ⓒ	Ⓓ		37.	Ⓐ	Ⓑ	Ⓒ	Ⓓ
12.	Ⓕ	Ⓖ	Ⓗ	Ⓙ		38.	Ⓕ	Ⓖ	Ⓗ	Ⓙ
13.	Ⓐ	Ⓑ	Ⓒ	Ⓓ		39.	Ⓐ	Ⓑ	Ⓒ	Ⓓ
14.	Ⓕ	Ⓖ	Ⓗ	Ⓙ		40.	Ⓕ	Ⓖ	Ⓗ	Ⓙ
15.	Ⓐ	Ⓑ	Ⓒ	Ⓓ		41.	Ⓐ	Ⓑ	Ⓒ	Ⓓ
16.	Ⓕ	Ⓖ	Ⓗ	Ⓙ		42.	Ⓕ	Ⓖ	Ⓗ	Ⓙ
17.	Ⓐ	Ⓑ	Ⓒ	Ⓓ		43.	Ⓐ	Ⓑ	Ⓒ	Ⓓ
18.	Ⓕ	Ⓖ	Ⓗ	Ⓙ		44.	Ⓕ	Ⓖ	Ⓗ	Ⓙ
19.	Ⓐ	Ⓑ	Ⓒ	Ⓓ		45.	Ⓐ	Ⓑ	Ⓒ	Ⓓ
20.	Ⓕ	Ⓖ	Ⓗ	Ⓙ		46.	Ⓕ	Ⓖ	Ⓗ	Ⓙ
21.	Ⓐ	Ⓑ	Ⓒ	Ⓓ		47.	Ⓐ	Ⓑ	Ⓒ	Ⓓ
22.	Ⓕ	Ⓖ	Ⓗ	Ⓙ		48.	Ⓕ	Ⓖ	Ⓗ	Ⓙ
23.	Ⓐ	Ⓑ	Ⓒ	Ⓓ		49.	Ⓐ	Ⓑ	Ⓒ	Ⓓ
24.	Ⓕ	Ⓖ	Ⓗ	Ⓙ		50.	Ⓕ	Ⓖ	Ⓗ	Ⓙ
25.	Ⓐ	Ⓑ	Ⓒ	Ⓓ		51.	Ⓐ	Ⓑ	Ⓒ	Ⓓ
26.	Ⓕ	Ⓖ	Ⓗ	Ⓙ		52.	Ⓕ	Ⓖ	Ⓗ	Ⓙ

Blank Grids for Gridded Responses

1.

2.

3.

4.

5.

6.

7.

8.

9.

10.

11.

12.

Student Answer Sheet: NAEP Practice Test

Multiple Choice

1.	Ⓐ	Ⓑ	Ⓒ	Ⓓ	Ⓔ
2.	Ⓐ	Ⓑ	Ⓒ	Ⓓ	Ⓔ
3.	Ⓐ	Ⓑ	Ⓒ	Ⓓ	Ⓔ
4.	Ⓐ	Ⓑ	Ⓒ	Ⓓ	Ⓔ
5.	Ⓐ	Ⓑ	Ⓒ	Ⓓ	Ⓔ
6.	Ⓐ	Ⓑ	Ⓒ	Ⓓ	Ⓔ
7.	Ⓐ	Ⓑ	Ⓒ	Ⓓ	Ⓔ
8.	Ⓐ	Ⓑ	Ⓒ	Ⓓ	Ⓔ
9.	Ⓐ	Ⓑ	Ⓒ	Ⓓ	Ⓔ
10.	Ⓐ	Ⓑ	Ⓒ	Ⓓ	Ⓔ
11.	Ⓐ	Ⓑ	Ⓒ	Ⓓ	Ⓔ
12.	Ⓐ	Ⓑ	Ⓒ	Ⓓ	Ⓔ
13.	Ⓐ	Ⓑ	Ⓒ	Ⓓ	Ⓔ
14.	Ⓐ	Ⓑ	Ⓒ	Ⓓ	Ⓔ
15.	Ⓐ	Ⓑ	Ⓒ	Ⓓ	Ⓔ
16.	Ⓐ	Ⓑ	Ⓒ	Ⓓ	Ⓔ
17.	Ⓐ	Ⓑ	Ⓒ	Ⓓ	Ⓔ
18.	Ⓐ	Ⓑ	Ⓒ	Ⓓ	Ⓔ
19.	Ⓐ	Ⓑ	Ⓒ	Ⓓ	Ⓔ
20.	Ⓐ	Ⓑ	Ⓒ	Ⓓ	Ⓔ
21.	Ⓐ	Ⓑ	Ⓒ	Ⓓ	Ⓔ
22.	Ⓐ	Ⓑ	Ⓒ	Ⓓ	Ⓔ
23.	Ⓐ	Ⓑ	Ⓒ	Ⓓ	Ⓔ
24.	Ⓐ	Ⓑ	Ⓒ	Ⓓ	Ⓔ
25.	Ⓐ	Ⓑ	Ⓒ	Ⓓ	Ⓔ
26.	Ⓐ	Ⓑ	Ⓒ	Ⓓ	Ⓔ
27.	Ⓐ	Ⓑ	Ⓒ	Ⓓ	Ⓔ
28.	Ⓐ	Ⓑ	Ⓒ	Ⓓ	Ⓔ
29.	Ⓐ	Ⓑ	Ⓒ	Ⓓ	Ⓔ
30.	Ⓐ	Ⓑ	Ⓒ	Ⓓ	Ⓔ
31.	Ⓐ	Ⓑ	Ⓒ	Ⓓ	Ⓔ
32.	Ⓐ	Ⓑ	Ⓒ	Ⓓ	Ⓔ
33.	Ⓐ	Ⓑ	Ⓒ	Ⓓ	Ⓔ
34.	Ⓐ	Ⓑ	Ⓒ	Ⓓ	Ⓔ
35.	Ⓐ	Ⓑ	Ⓒ	Ⓓ	Ⓔ
36.	Ⓐ	Ⓑ	Ⓒ	Ⓓ	Ⓔ
37.	Ⓐ	Ⓑ	Ⓒ	Ⓓ	Ⓔ
38.	Ⓐ	Ⓑ	Ⓒ	Ⓓ	Ⓔ
39.	Ⓐ	Ⓑ	Ⓒ	Ⓓ	Ⓔ
40.	Ⓐ	Ⓑ	Ⓒ	Ⓓ	Ⓔ
41.	Ⓐ	Ⓑ	Ⓒ	Ⓓ	Ⓔ
42.	Ⓐ	Ⓑ	Ⓒ	Ⓓ	Ⓔ
43.	Ⓐ	Ⓑ	Ⓒ	Ⓓ	Ⓔ
44.	Ⓐ	Ⓑ	Ⓒ	Ⓓ	Ⓔ
45.	Ⓐ	Ⓑ	Ⓒ	Ⓓ	Ⓔ
46.	Ⓐ	Ⓑ	Ⓒ	Ⓓ	Ⓔ
47.	Ⓐ	Ⓑ	Ⓒ	Ⓓ	Ⓔ
48.	Ⓐ	Ⓑ	Ⓒ	Ⓓ	Ⓔ
49.	Ⓐ	Ⓑ	Ⓒ	Ⓓ	Ⓔ
50.	Ⓐ	Ⓑ	Ⓒ	Ⓓ	Ⓔ
51.	Ⓐ	Ⓑ	Ⓒ	Ⓓ	Ⓔ
52.	Ⓐ	Ⓑ	Ⓒ	Ⓓ	Ⓔ

Go On

Student Answer Sheet: NAEP Practice Test (continued)

53.	Ⓐ	Ⓑ	Ⓒ	Ⓓ	Ⓔ
54.	Ⓐ	Ⓑ	Ⓒ	Ⓓ	Ⓔ
55.	Ⓐ	Ⓑ	Ⓒ	Ⓓ	Ⓔ
56.	Ⓐ	Ⓑ	Ⓒ	Ⓓ	Ⓔ
57.	Ⓐ	Ⓑ	Ⓒ	Ⓓ	Ⓔ
58.	Ⓐ	Ⓑ	Ⓒ	Ⓓ	Ⓔ
59.	Ⓐ	Ⓑ	Ⓒ	Ⓓ	Ⓔ
60.	Ⓐ	Ⓑ	Ⓒ	Ⓓ	Ⓔ
61.	Ⓐ	Ⓑ	Ⓒ	Ⓓ	Ⓔ
62.	Ⓐ	Ⓑ	Ⓒ	Ⓓ	Ⓔ
63.	Ⓐ	Ⓑ	Ⓒ	Ⓓ	Ⓔ

Short Constructed Response

64. Short Constructed Response

65. Short Constructed Response

66. Short Constructed Response

67. Short Constructed Response

Extended Constructed Response

68. Extended Constructed Response

69. Extended Constructed Response

70. Extended Constructed Response

Student Answer Sheet: SAT 10 Practice Test

Mathematics: Problem Solving

1. (A) (B) (C) (D)
2. (F) (G) (H) (J)
3. (A) (B) (C) (D)
4. (F) (G) (H) (J)
5. (A) (B) (C) (D)
6. (F) (G) (H) (J)
7. (A) (B) (C) (D)
8. (F) (G) (H) (J)
9. (A) (B) (C) (D)
10. (F) (G) (H) (J)
11. (A) (B) (C) (D)
12. (F) (G) (H) (J)
13. (A) (B) (C) (D)
14. (F) (G) (H) (J)
15. (A) (B) (C) (D)
16. (F) (G) (H) (J)
17. (A) (B) (C) (D)
18. (F) (G) (H) (J)
19. (A) (B) (C) (D)
20. (F) (G) (H) (J)
21. (A) (B) (C) (D)
22. (F) (G) (H) (J)
23. (A) (B) (C) (D)
24. (F) (G) (H) (J)
25. (A) (B) (C) (D)

26. (F) (G) (H) (J)
27. (A) (B) (C) (D)
28. (F) (G) (H) (J)
29. (A) (B) (C) (D)
30. (F) (G) (H) (J)
31. (A) (B) (C) (D)
32. (F) (G) (H) (J)
33. (A) (B) (C) (D)
34. (F) (G) (H) (J)
35. (A) (B) (C) (D)
36. (F) (G) (H) (J)
37. (A) (B) (C) (D)
38. (F) (G) (H) (J)
39. (A) (B) (C) (D)
40. (F) (G) (H) (J)
41. (A) (B) (C) (D)
42. (F) (G) (H) (J)
43. (A) (B) (C) (D)
44. (F) (G) (H) (J)
45. (A) (B) (C) (D)
46. (F) (G) (H) (J)
47. (A) (B) (C) (D)
48. (F) (G) (H) (J)
49. (A) (B) (C) (D)
50. (F) (G) (H) (J)

Go On

Student Answer Sheet: SAT 10 Practice Test (continued)

Mathematics: Procedures

1. Ⓐ Ⓑ Ⓒ Ⓓ Ⓔ
2. Ⓕ Ⓖ Ⓗ Ⓙ Ⓚ
3. Ⓐ Ⓑ Ⓒ Ⓓ Ⓔ
4. Ⓕ Ⓖ Ⓗ Ⓙ Ⓚ
5. Ⓐ Ⓑ Ⓒ Ⓓ Ⓔ
6. Ⓕ Ⓖ Ⓗ Ⓙ Ⓚ
7. Ⓐ Ⓑ Ⓒ Ⓓ Ⓔ
8. Ⓕ Ⓖ Ⓗ Ⓙ Ⓚ
9. Ⓐ Ⓑ Ⓒ Ⓓ Ⓔ
10. Ⓕ Ⓖ Ⓗ Ⓙ Ⓚ
11. Ⓐ Ⓑ Ⓒ Ⓓ Ⓔ
12. Ⓕ Ⓖ Ⓗ Ⓙ Ⓚ
13. Ⓐ Ⓑ Ⓒ Ⓓ Ⓔ
14. Ⓕ Ⓖ Ⓗ Ⓙ Ⓚ
15. Ⓐ Ⓑ Ⓒ Ⓓ Ⓔ

16. Ⓕ Ⓖ Ⓗ Ⓙ Ⓚ
17. Ⓐ Ⓑ Ⓒ Ⓓ Ⓔ
18. Ⓕ Ⓖ Ⓗ Ⓙ Ⓚ
19. Ⓐ Ⓑ Ⓒ Ⓓ Ⓔ
20. Ⓕ Ⓖ Ⓗ Ⓙ Ⓚ
21. Ⓐ Ⓑ Ⓒ Ⓓ Ⓔ
22. Ⓕ Ⓖ Ⓗ Ⓙ Ⓚ
23. Ⓐ Ⓑ Ⓒ Ⓓ Ⓔ
24. Ⓕ Ⓖ Ⓗ Ⓙ Ⓚ
25. Ⓐ Ⓑ Ⓒ Ⓓ Ⓔ
26. Ⓕ Ⓖ Ⓗ Ⓙ Ⓚ
27. Ⓐ Ⓑ Ⓒ Ⓓ Ⓔ
28. Ⓕ Ⓖ Ⓗ Ⓙ Ⓚ
29. Ⓐ Ⓑ Ⓒ Ⓓ Ⓔ
30. Ⓕ Ⓖ Ⓗ Ⓙ Ⓚ

Student Answer Sheet: ITBS Practice Test

•••

Multiple Choice

1. Ⓐ Ⓑ Ⓒ Ⓓ   21. Ⓐ Ⓑ Ⓒ Ⓓ

2. Ⓕ Ⓖ Ⓗ Ⓙ   22. Ⓕ Ⓖ Ⓗ Ⓙ

3. Ⓐ Ⓑ Ⓒ Ⓓ   23. Ⓐ Ⓑ Ⓒ Ⓓ

4. Ⓕ Ⓖ Ⓗ Ⓙ   24. Ⓕ Ⓖ Ⓗ Ⓙ

5. Ⓐ Ⓑ Ⓒ Ⓓ   25. Ⓐ Ⓑ Ⓒ Ⓓ

6. Ⓕ Ⓖ Ⓗ Ⓙ   26. Ⓕ Ⓖ Ⓗ Ⓙ

7. Ⓐ Ⓑ Ⓒ Ⓓ   27. Ⓐ Ⓑ Ⓒ Ⓓ

8. Ⓕ Ⓖ Ⓗ Ⓙ   28. Ⓕ Ⓖ Ⓗ Ⓙ

9. Ⓐ Ⓑ Ⓒ Ⓓ   29. Ⓐ Ⓑ Ⓒ Ⓓ

10. Ⓕ Ⓖ Ⓗ Ⓙ   30. Ⓕ Ⓖ Ⓗ Ⓙ

11. Ⓐ Ⓑ Ⓒ Ⓓ   31. Ⓐ Ⓑ Ⓒ Ⓓ

12. Ⓕ Ⓖ Ⓗ Ⓙ   32. Ⓕ Ⓖ Ⓗ Ⓙ

13. Ⓐ Ⓑ Ⓒ Ⓓ   33. Ⓐ Ⓑ Ⓒ Ⓓ

14. Ⓕ Ⓖ Ⓗ Ⓙ   34. Ⓕ Ⓖ Ⓗ Ⓙ

15. Ⓐ Ⓑ Ⓒ Ⓓ   35. Ⓐ Ⓑ Ⓒ Ⓓ

16. Ⓕ Ⓖ Ⓗ Ⓙ   36. Ⓕ Ⓖ Ⓗ Ⓙ

17. Ⓐ Ⓑ Ⓒ Ⓓ   37. Ⓐ Ⓑ Ⓒ Ⓓ

18. Ⓕ Ⓖ Ⓗ Ⓙ   38. Ⓕ Ⓖ Ⓗ Ⓙ

19. Ⓐ Ⓑ Ⓒ Ⓓ   39. Ⓐ Ⓑ Ⓒ Ⓓ

20. Ⓕ Ⓖ Ⓗ Ⓙ   40. Ⓕ Ⓖ Ⓗ Ⓙ

Name_____ Class_____ Date_____

Student Answer Sheet: TerraNova Practice Test

Part 1

1. Ⓐ Ⓑ Ⓒ Ⓓ Ⓔ
2. Ⓕ Ⓖ Ⓗ Ⓙ Ⓚ
3. Ⓐ Ⓑ Ⓒ Ⓓ Ⓔ
4. Ⓕ Ⓖ Ⓗ Ⓙ Ⓚ
5. Ⓐ Ⓑ Ⓒ Ⓓ Ⓔ
6. Ⓕ Ⓖ Ⓗ Ⓙ Ⓚ
7. Ⓐ Ⓑ Ⓒ Ⓓ Ⓔ
8. Ⓕ Ⓖ Ⓗ Ⓙ
9. Ⓐ Ⓑ Ⓒ Ⓓ
10. Ⓕ Ⓖ Ⓗ Ⓙ
11. Ⓐ Ⓑ Ⓒ Ⓓ
12. Ⓕ Ⓖ Ⓗ Ⓙ
13. Ⓐ Ⓑ Ⓒ Ⓓ
14. Ⓕ Ⓖ Ⓗ Ⓙ
15. Ⓐ Ⓑ Ⓒ Ⓓ
16. Ⓕ Ⓖ Ⓗ Ⓙ
17. Ⓐ Ⓑ Ⓒ Ⓓ

Part 2

18. Ⓕ Ⓖ Ⓗ Ⓙ
19. Ⓐ Ⓑ Ⓒ Ⓓ
20. Ⓕ Ⓖ Ⓗ Ⓙ
21. Ⓐ Ⓑ Ⓒ Ⓓ
22. Ⓕ Ⓖ Ⓗ Ⓙ
23. Ⓐ Ⓑ Ⓒ Ⓓ
24. Ⓕ Ⓖ Ⓗ Ⓙ
25. Ⓐ Ⓑ Ⓒ Ⓓ
26. Ⓕ Ⓖ Ⓗ Ⓙ
27. Ⓐ Ⓑ Ⓒ Ⓓ
28. Ⓕ Ⓖ Ⓗ Ⓙ

29. Ⓐ Ⓑ Ⓒ Ⓓ
30. Ⓕ Ⓖ Ⓗ Ⓙ
31. Ⓐ Ⓑ Ⓒ Ⓓ
32. Ⓕ Ⓖ Ⓗ Ⓙ
33. Ⓐ Ⓑ Ⓒ Ⓓ
34. Ⓕ Ⓖ Ⓗ Ⓙ
35. Ⓐ Ⓑ Ⓒ Ⓓ
36. Ⓕ Ⓖ Ⓗ Ⓙ
37. Ⓐ Ⓑ Ⓒ Ⓓ
38. Ⓕ Ⓖ Ⓗ Ⓙ
39. Ⓐ Ⓑ Ⓒ Ⓓ
40. Ⓕ Ⓖ Ⓗ Ⓙ
41. Ⓐ Ⓑ Ⓒ Ⓓ
42. Ⓕ Ⓖ Ⓗ Ⓙ
43. Ⓐ Ⓑ Ⓒ Ⓓ
44. Ⓕ Ⓖ Ⓗ Ⓙ
45. Ⓐ Ⓑ Ⓒ Ⓓ
46. Ⓕ Ⓖ Ⓗ Ⓙ
47. Ⓐ Ⓑ Ⓒ Ⓓ
48. Ⓕ Ⓖ Ⓗ Ⓙ
49. Ⓐ Ⓑ Ⓒ Ⓓ
50. Ⓕ Ⓖ Ⓗ Ⓙ
51. Ⓐ Ⓑ Ⓒ Ⓓ
52. Ⓕ Ⓖ Ⓗ Ⓙ
53. Ⓐ Ⓑ Ⓒ Ⓓ
54. Ⓕ Ⓖ Ⓗ Ⓙ
55. Ⓐ Ⓑ Ⓒ Ⓓ
56. Ⓕ Ⓖ Ⓗ Ⓙ

Go On

Student Answer Sheet: TerraNova Practice Test
(continued)

Part 3

1. Ⓐ Ⓑ Ⓒ Ⓓ Ⓔ
2. Ⓕ Ⓖ Ⓗ Ⓙ Ⓚ
3. Ⓐ Ⓑ Ⓒ Ⓓ Ⓔ
4. Ⓕ Ⓖ Ⓗ Ⓙ Ⓚ
5. Ⓐ Ⓑ Ⓒ Ⓓ Ⓔ
6. Ⓕ Ⓖ Ⓗ Ⓙ Ⓚ
7. Ⓐ Ⓑ Ⓒ Ⓓ Ⓔ
8. Ⓕ Ⓖ Ⓗ Ⓙ Ⓚ
9. Ⓐ Ⓑ Ⓒ Ⓓ Ⓔ
10. Ⓕ Ⓖ Ⓗ Ⓙ Ⓚ
11. Ⓐ Ⓑ Ⓒ Ⓓ Ⓔ
12. Ⓕ Ⓖ Ⓗ Ⓙ Ⓚ
13. Ⓐ Ⓑ Ⓒ Ⓓ Ⓔ
14. Ⓕ Ⓖ Ⓗ Ⓙ Ⓚ
15. Ⓐ Ⓑ Ⓒ Ⓓ Ⓔ
16. Ⓕ Ⓖ Ⓗ Ⓙ Ⓚ
17. Ⓐ Ⓑ Ⓒ Ⓓ Ⓔ
18. Ⓕ Ⓖ Ⓗ Ⓙ Ⓚ
19. Ⓐ Ⓑ Ⓒ Ⓓ Ⓔ
20. Ⓕ Ⓖ Ⓗ Ⓙ Ⓚ